ግጥሞቼና ትዝታዎቼ

My Poems and Memory Notes

ፈቃዱ ፉላስ

Fekadu Fullas

ግጥሞቼና ትዝታዎቼ

My Poems and Memory Notes

ከፈቃዱ ፉላስ
By Fekadu Fullas

2012 (ኢ.ኢ.ኢ.)/ 2020 (G.C.)
USA

ግጥሞቼና ትዝታዎቼ My Poems and Memory Notes
ፈቃዱ ፉላስ Fekadu Fullas

Copyright © 2020/ 2012 Fekadu Fullas

All rights reserved. No part of this book protected by this copyright notice may be reproduced or utilized in any form by any means, electronic or mechanical, including photocopying, recording or by any information storage and retrieval system , without prior written consent from the copyright owner.

ማውጫ (Table of Contents)

ምስጋና --- 1
መቅድም --- 2

ክፍል 1 (Part 1): የአማርኛ ግጥሞች

ራዕይ --- 5
ተስፋ --- 6
ሽርሽር በአንድ ምሽት ጨረቃ------------------------------------ 7
የግጥም ዛር ሲነሳ-- 8
ግጥም ስለ ግጥም--- 9
ለሳይንስ አፍቃሪዎች--- 10
ገጣሚ ሲነሳ-- 11
መርካቶ--አዲስ አበባ--- 12
ለገጣሚ ከበደች ተክለአብ --------------------------------------- 14
የታቦት ቀን ትዝታ --- 15
ጨለማና ብርሃን --- 16
የሃገር ትዝታ/ ስሜት -- 17
የሃዋዩ አሳተ ገሞራ (Hawaii) -------------------------------- 19
ባህረ ግጥም -- 20
የጽጌረዳ አበባ ምሥጢር --------------------------------------- 21
ከበር ሲመታ በሃዘን በደስታ ----------------------------------- 22
ፀሐይ ሲዘንብ (የዘንድሮ ሙቀት) ----------------------------- 23
የወንድም (ዘነበ ፉላስ) ፍቅር ---------------------------------- 24
የተስፋ ጭላንጭል--- 26
የሳይንቲስቱ ውሎ--- 28
የእፀዋት ጥቅም--- 31

በሁለት እግር የቆመ ስሜት	33
ቀንና ሌሊት	34
አይ የፍርድ ነገር	35
ተፈራራቂ ስሜት (ፍልስፍና)	36
ድልድዩ ሲቋረጥ	37
የዝምታ ትርጉም	39
ጎሰኝነት (የፖለቲካ አስተያየት)	40
የምዕራብ ሃገሮች በጋና ክረምት ሹዋሹዌ	41
ሞትና ሕይወት	43
ስለሙዚቃ/ዘፈን	44
ፍቅር ምንድነው?	45
መደመር (የለውጥ ነፋስ)	46
ህክምና በግጥም ዓይን	47
ቁም ነገርና ቀልድ	49
ተስፋ	50
የኢትዮጵያ ትንሳኤ	51
ቀስት ደመና - ኢትዮጵያ	52
የሃገር ፍቅር	54
ጎሰኝነት	55
የወጣትነት ዘመን	56
ይብላኝ ለሻሸመኔ	58
የባህል መድኃኒት በግጥም መልክ	59
ዕንቁጣጣሽ	60
የቡራዩው መዓት	61
የድሮ--የእህቶቼን ሠርግ ሳስታውስ የተጻፈ	62
የምድጃ እሳት ዳር ጨዋታ	63
ዑደተ ጊዜ	64
ስሜት	65
የእውቀት ማዕድ ግብዣ	66

ከለገባፎ ለተፈናቀሉ ------------------------------------	67
የተስፋ መደብዘዝ ------------------------------------	68
የተከሰከሰው EAL ቦይንግ 737 ማክስ 8 (በረራ ቁጥር 302)--	69
የኢትዮጵያ ዕንቆቅልሽ -------------------------------	70
የኮድ ብሉ (Code Blue) ነፍስ አድን ጥሪ -------------	71
የኛ ዘመን፣ የኛ ጊዜ -------------------------------	74
የኢትዮጵያ ሀኪሞች ጥያቄ --------------------------	75
በ ICU የሚታይ መደበኛ ትዕይንት -------------------	76
ሀኪሙ ሲታመም ----------------------------------	78
የማይሞት ተስፋ ---------------------------------	79
ደመና ስጋልብ ---------------------------------	80
የብራዚሉ (የአማዞኑ) እሳት ------------------------	81
የግጥም ሃይል ----------------------------------	82
ለሺካጎ የድነረ ምረቅ ትምህርት አስተማሪዬ (NRF) ----	83
የብዕርና የሕይወት ጉዞ -----------------------------	84
መወድስ ለሳይንቲስቶች -----------------------------	85
የኮሮና ወረርሽኝን ለሚታገሉ -------------------------	86

Part 2: Poems in English

Day and Night -------------------------------------- 88
On the Paradox of Love --------------------------- 89
New Year --- 91
Tribute to Facebook ----------------------------- 93
Sunrise and Sunset ------------------------------- 94
On a Day the Sun Rains ------------------------- 95
Heroes and Heroines of COVID-19 ----------- 96

Part 3: Memory Notes

Newsmen of Yester year ---------------------- 99
One rainy night in Addis Ababa ------------- 101
The Afro-hair styled Gate-man (*Gofer*) ---------- 103
Parents' Day ----------------------------------- 105
The *Pari Mode* Era --------------------------- 107
Epiphany (*Timqet*) --------------------------- 109
Ethiopian New Year (*Enqutatash*) ----------- 111
Tarzan -- 114
Yeneta Zeleqe ------------------------------- 116
Of an Old Wedding -------------------------- 119
Of *Gesho Terra* ------------------------------ 123
Qirtcha and *Figna* ----------------------------- 125
Senbete --------------------------------------- 127
The Abortive Coup d'état of G Mengistu Neway 129
Studying in Churches and at Cemeteries ---------- 132
Gizaw the Robin-hood ---------------------- 135
Mud-slinging (*Chiqa Wurwera*) ------------------ 137

Of *Wolde Pastae Bet*	139
The day I lost the Coffee Beans	140
The Primers and March of Time	142
The Mill House (*Wefcho Bet*)	143
Of Parties	145
Sugar (*Wonji Sikuar*)	146
Kur Kur	147
Speaking of Siberia	148
Tea rooms	149
Amin Hanna	150
The Camping Tent	152
Honey wine Houses	154

ምስጋና

ይህን መጽሐፍ ለእትመት ለማብቃት ባደረግሁት ጥረት ለረዱኝ መልካም ሰዎች ምስጋና ለማቅረብ እሻለሁ።

ፕ/ር አቻምየለህ ደበላ የመጽሐፉን ሽፋን ምስል ስላዘጋጃልኝ ምስጋናዬ የላቀ ነው። ምስሉ የያዘውን ሐሳብ በእንግሊዝኛ ቋንቋ እንዲህ ሲል ገልጸታል፤ «[The] cover design is about memories of earlier years and some kept in a Mudai [traditional hand–woven small embroidered basket] like a jewel and a life symbolized by dark and light expressed with words that express [reflect] views personal and yet universal.» ገላጭ ቃል ነው።

ረዳት ፕ/ር ከበደች ተክለአብ ያልተቋረጠ የሐሳብ ድጋፍ ስለለገሰችኝ ባለውለታዬ ናት። መላውን ረቂቅ አንብባ ጠቃሚ ማስተካከያዎችን እንዳካትት ስለረዳችኝ የመጨረሻው ውጤት ከመጀመሪያው ረቂቅ በተሻለ ሁኔታ ሊቀርብ ችሏል።

በአካል አግኝቼው ባላውቅም አቶ ዳንኤል አበራ ለሥነ ጽሑፍ ካለው ፍቅር የተነሳ እራሱም ደራሲ በመሆኑ ይህ መጽሐፍ እንዲታተም ውድ ጊዜውን ቸሮኛል። የእርሱ አርታኢነት፤ ጠቃሚ አስተያየቶችና ቴክኒካዊ እርዳታ ባይታከልበት ኖሮ መጽሐፉን ለእትመት ማድረስ አስቸጋሪ ይሆን ነበር።

እንዲሁም አንዳንዶቹን ግጥሞቼንና የትዝታ ማስታወሻዎቼን በማንበብሰብ ማጎደረ መረጃ ላይ ያነበቡ በርከት ያሉ ሰዎች ይህን መጽሐፍ እንዳዘጋጅ ስላበረታቱኝ ምስጋናዬ ይድረሳቸው።

መቅድም

«ግጥሞቼና ትዝታዎቼ»ን እነሆ! ይህን ድርሰት እንድጽፍ ያነሳሳኝ ዋናው ምክንያት በተለያየ ጊዜያት የተሰሙኝን ጥልቅ ስሜቶች በግጥም መልክ ለመግለጽና ዘወትር በሐሳቤ ብቅ ጥልቅ የሚሉትን የልጅነትና የወጣትነት ትዝታዎቼን በቋሚነት ለማስተላለፍ ነው። በአንድ ወቅት ኢ.ኢ.ዲ.ን (EEDN [Ethiopian Electronic Distribution Network]) በተባለ የመወያያ አውታረ መረብ ላይ ትዝታዎቼን በተከታታይ በጽሑፍ አጋራ ነበር። ከዚያም ያንኑ አካሄድ በመቀጠልና እንዲሁም ግጥሞቼን በመጨመር በፌስቡክ ግድግዳዬ ላይ መለጠፍ ጀመርኩ። ጽሑፎቼን ያነበቡ ጥቂት ሰዎች በመጽሐፍ መልክ ቢዘጋጅ ጥሩ ይሆናል የሚል አስተያየት ሰነዘሩ። እኔም ምክራቸውን በመቀበል ለመጀመሪያ ጊዜ ጉዳዩን ትኩረት ሰጥቼ አሰብኩበት። ይህ መድብል የዚያ ሐሳብ ውጤት ነው።

የአማርኛና እንግሊዝኛ ግጥሞችን እንዲሁም በእንግሊዝኛ የተደረሱ ትዝታዎችን በአንድ መጽሐፍ ማካተት ጉራማይሌ ቢያስመስለውም፣ ለዚህ መጽሐፍ ያንኑ አቀራረብ መረጥኩ። የአማርኛ ግጥሞችን ወደ እንግሊዝኛ መተርጎም የሚቻል ቢሆንም፣ ይዘቱንና መልኩን መጠበቅ አስቸጋሪ ይሆናል። በሌላ በኩል፣ ቀደም ሲል ትዝታዎቼን በእንግሊዝኛ መጻፍ ስለጀመርኩ፣ በመሃል ወደ አማርኛ መተርጎሙን አስፈላጊ ሆኖ አላገኘሁትም። ለነገሩስ የዚህ መጽሐፍ አብዛኛው አንባቢያን ሁለቱንም ቋንቋዎች ማንበብና መረዳት እንደሚችሉ መገመት ይቻላል። በነዚህ ምክንያቶች የተነሳ መጽሐፉ በዚህ መልክ ተዘጋጀ።

ከቁስ ትምህርት ቤት (ከፊደል ቆጠራ እስከ ዳዊት መድገም)፣ ከኛ እስከ 12ኛ ክፍል እንግሊዝኛ ት/ቤት፣ ቀጥሎም በቀ.ኃ.ሥ. ዩኒቨርሲቲ ከኛ ዓመት በላይ የዘለቀ የአማርኛ ቋንቋ ትምህርት የለኝም (ከዚያ ወደ ሳይንስ ዓለም ነው የገባሁት)፤ ነገር ግን ሁልጊዜም ሥነ ጽሑፍ ይስበኝ ነበር። በተለይም በተዋበ ቋንቋ የሚጻፉ የአማርኛም ሆኑ የእንግሊዝኛ ጽሑፎች ማንበብ ያረካኝ ነበር። ስድ ንባብ ወይም ግጥም፣ ሐሳብን በቀላሉ

አንዳንዴም በጥልቀት ለመግለጽ የሚረዳ ዓይነተኛ መሣሪያ ነው። እኔም ይህንኑ ለመሞከር ተነሳሁ።

ትዝታዎቼ ብዙ ዓመታት ወደኋላ በምናብ ተመልሼ የጻፍኳቸው በመሆናቸው ግድፈት ቢኖራቸው ጎላልነቱን ስህተቱ የኔ ብቻ ይሆናል።

መልካም ንባብ ይሁንላችሁ።
****

ፈቃዱ ፉላስ፣ ፒ.ኤች.ዲ. (PhD)
2012 (2020)

ክፍል 1 (Part 1)

የአማርኛ ግጥሞች

ራዕይ

ዛሬ አለን ስንል ሳናውቀው ነገን
ከነገ ባሻገር ስንቃኝ ዓመታትን
ከቶ ምን ይሆን የሚጠብቀን?

ግና እንኑር ዛሬ በሚታየን ፀዳል
ይፍሰስ በልባችን የተስፋ ማዕበል።

ጮራው ይፈንጠቅ ወጥቶ ከእምቁ እሳት
ሁሌም ያበራ ዘንድ የሌሎችን ስሜት።

ዕውቀት ይጓዝ ይንደድ ከአእምሮ እንበርት ወጥቶ
እንደ ጅረት ይፍሰስ ያለገደብ ሞልቶ።

ክናዳችን ይሁን መብረሪያ አክናፋት
መላው መንፈሳችን ያርግ ከሰማያት።

አድማሳችን እፉቅ መንገዳችን ብርሃን
እንደርስበታለን ጨለማን ገላልጠን።

ሚችና ፈራሽ ነን ቀኑ የመጣ ዕለት
ዛሬን ግን እንኑር በሃሴት በትጋት።   (09 May 2018)

ተስፋ

በጎዋው ላይ እንደሚወረወር ኮከብ
ብልጭ ድርግም እያለ ሲስብ ቀልብ

ይህ ብሩህ ተስፋ ከቶ የማይዳስስ የማይደረስ
እንደ ውልብልቢት ከሩቅ ብቻ የሚርመሰመስ

ረቂቅ አሊያም ግዙፍ ሆኖ
በሁለት አልባሳት ተጀቡኖ

ቀኑ መች ይሆን ተገልጦ የሚታየው?
ተስፋው እውን የሚሆነው
ሰቆቃው አልፎ ሀሴት የሚነግሠው።   (11 May 2018)

ሽርሽር በአንድ ምሽት ጨረቃ
(በሚዞሪ ወንዝ ዳርቻ)

እግሬን ላውጣ ብዬ ጥቂት ልንሸራሸር
በምሽት ጨረቃ ሄድኩኝ ከወንዝ ዳር።

ተከትዬ ስጓዝ የወንዙን ዳርቻ
ፀጥ ባለው ምሽት በማይኖረው አቻ

ማተርኩ ወደ ሰማይ ልቃኝ ከዋክብትን
ከአጽናፍ እስከ አጽናፍ የተበተኑትን

ግና ጎልቶ ታየኝ የጨረቃ ድምቀት
ያ የብርሃን ምጣድ ተንጣሎ በውበት።

ሲታይ ገዘፏ፤ ደምቆ ከምድር ተጠግቶ
በእጅ ያዘው ያሰኛል ልብን አሸፍቶ።   (14 May 2018)

የግጥም ዛር ሲነሳ

የግጥም ዛር ሲነሳ እንደ ወንዙ ዳር ሳቢሳ
ወደ ሰማያት ከንፎ ሲመለስ ለምድር አሥሣ

ሐረግ መዞ ቤቱን ሠርቶ
በሥርዓት አሳምሮ አበጃጅቶ
ገጣጥሞ አዘጋጅቶ ለድግሱ
ግቡ ይላል ከማዕዱ ተቀደሱ፡፡

እንደ አዶ ከበሬ አይዞህ ሲባል፤ ብርታ ሲባል
በከበሮ ሲደምቅ በጭብጨባ ሲግል
ዶቃና አምባር ሲያቃጭል እንደ ደወል

እጣን ሲጨስ ብርጉድ ሲነድ
ሸቱው ሰፈስ ቤቱን ሲያውድ

ስሜት ሲግል ክህሎት ሲታወቅ
ግጥም እንደ እሳተ-ገሞራ
ይፍሰስ ይፍለቅለቅ፡፡

ያኔ ይወጣል የግጥም መክሊቱ
እንደ ባሕር ሱናሚ ደርሶ ከምድሪቱ
ከቶ የማያቆሙት፤ የማያግቱቱ፡፡ (12 May, 2018)

ግጥም ስለ ግጥም

የሥነ ቃል ውበት የማይጠወልገው
በጊዜ እልፈት ከቶ የማይወረዛው
በቃለ-ቀለማት ደምቆና አሽብርቆ
ግጥምም ይሳላል በምናብ ሸራ ላይ
ረቅቆ! ልቆ! መጥቆ።

ከጥጥ ፍሬ ይውጡ ቃላት ተፈልቅቀው
ተፈትልው ተዳውረው
ባለ ኅብረ ቀለም ድርና ማግ ሆነው
ይግቡ ከልባችን አእምሮአችንን ሠርፀው።   (09 May, 2018)

ለሳይንስ አፍቃሪዎች

የሕይወት መፍቻ ቁልፍ የተፈጥሮ ሳይንስ
ሁልጊዜም ይደንቃል የዚህ ጥበብ አድማስ።

ጠልቆ፣ መጥቆ፣ ረቆ፣ ሐሳብን ሰቅዞ
እንደ ወንዝ ይፈሳል ሳያቋርጥ ጉዞ።

ሁለት አምሳል ይዞ በሁለት ገጽታ
ተስማምቶ፣ ወይ ተጣርሶ ችግርን ሊፈታ
ሳይንስ ይራመዳል ሳያቆም ላንዳፍታ።

አንደኛው ገጽታ ሕይወትን ሊያሻሽል፣ ሰዎችን ሊረዳ
ሁለተኛው ደግሞ ሳያቅደውና ሳያውቀው ሊጎዳ
ይነጉዳል ወደፊት ለማይቀረው ዕዳ።

ግን--
መነሻው ትክክል የታጀበ በዕውቀት
ከቶ የማይፋለስ መከታው «ምክንያት»
መድረሻውን ያውቃል አስቀድሞ ከፊት።

አይዞህ በርታ በሉት ከቶ አታመንታ
እንጠብቅሃለን ከጎጂ ቱማታ።

ትጋ ቀጥል «ሳይንስ» በያዝከው ጎዳና
በቀደድከው ፈለግ ባበራኸው ፋና።   (15 May 2018)

ገጣሚ ሲኖሳ

ለካስ ኃያል ነው ግጥም
ሐሳብን ሲገልጽ ያለ ድካም
ቃላቱም እንደ አሸን ይፈላል
እንደ ብርሃን ያበራል
እንድ ነጎድጓድ ያስተጋባል።
ያ የልጅነቱ፣ የሥነ ጽሑፍ ፍቅሩ
ገንፍሎ ወጥቷል ምሥጢሩ።

ለዘመናት የታመቀው ከህሎቱ
ተከፈተ በሩ፣ ተነሳ ስሜቱ።
ገና ይፈልቃል፣ ይፍለቀለቃል
የግጥም ግድቡ ተንዷል! ፈርሷል። (May 2018)

መርካቶ - አዲስ አበባ

አንች መርካቶ፣ አዲሳባ
የልጅነት የፍቅር አምባ
ያደግሁብሽ፣ የቦረቅሁብሽ
ኧረ እንዴት ነሽ?
እንደምነሽ?

ትዝታና ናፍቆቴን ይዤ
በምናብ መንኮራኩር ተጉዤ
እኔ እዚህ አንቺ እዚያ
ተለያይተን በምድር ዛቢያ
ፍቅራችን ሳይበርድ ሳይቀዘቅዝ
ሆኖኝ የማያልቅ ሥንቅና ጓዝ

ዓመታትና ርቀት ሳይገድቡን
እንኖራለን በናፍቆት
እንቀዝፋለን ኑሮን፣ እንጓዛለን በድፍረት፡፡

ያንቺ አድባር በዋልኩበት
ተከትሎኝ በኖርኩበት
በርታ ብላቴና እያልሽኝ
በመንፈስ እያበረታታሽኝ

አይዞህ እያልሽ ከጎኔ ሆነሽ
ዛሬም ነገም በጎሊናዬ ሰርፀሽ

ብርታቴ ኃይሌ አንችው ነሽ
ታንኳዬን ስቀዝፍ በፍቅርሽ፡፡

እናም መንፈሴ ይጠነክራል በምልዓት
ልጅነቴን አንቺን ሳስብ ቀን ከሌት

ዛሬስ የለሽም ይሉኛል፤ መልክሽ ጠቁሮ ተቀይሯል
ሙች ጊዜ ባለበት ይቆማል፤
ግና ይራመዳል-ይሄዳል-ይነጉዳል።

ሆኖም በኔ ዓይን፤ የያኔው የድሮው መልክሽ
ዘላለም ይኖራል ፍቅርሽ
የማይጠወልገው አካልሽ።

መርካቶ አዲሳባ
የፍቅር የትዝታ አምባ።   (18 May 2018)

ገጣሚ ከበደች ተክለአብ

ግጥም ከብዕርሽ ጫፍ ሲፈልቅ
እንደ ፏፏቴ ሲወርድ ሲፍለቀለቅ
በሐሳብ ሽራ ላይ ተነድፎ
ረቂቅ ሕይወትን በቃላት አግዝፎ
ደምቆ ፈክቶ፣ በቀለም ጎብር ዳብሮ
ይመታል ግጥምሽ የልብን ከበሮ።
ምቱን ሊያበረታ ሊያግል ትርታውን
ከዚያም አካልን ቀጥሎም አእምሮን
ምንድነው ግጥም ያለ ቃል ውበት
ያለ ጥልቀት፣ ያለ ቅርፅ፣ ያለ ይዘት?
የት ላይ ይሆን ድምቀቱ፣ ምን ይሆን ትርጉሙ?
በሕግጋት ብቻ ታጥሮ ዘውትር መዋተት መድከሙ።
ደንብስ ይኑር ሥነ ሥርዓት፣ ሕገ ግጥም
ይበልጣል ግን ይዘት - ቀለም - ጣዕም።

እቴ ያንቺ ግን እንደ ጣይ ያበራል
ከመቅረዙ መሃል ፈልቆ ብርሃን ይረጫል
የግጥምን ጮራ ይፈነጥቃል።
እንደ ጽጌረዳ እንቡጥ ይደምቃል
የሕይወት ተመክሮን ሳይሰለቸው በቃላት ይስላል።

ምናብ-ሰቃችሁ ቃል-ቀለሙን ጠብቆ
በጊዜ ቅርበት ወይም ርቀት ጣሙን ሳይለቅ ደምቆ
ቀን ሳይሸረው ሳያመክነው
ውብቱን ሳያጠውልግ ሳይቀንሰው
ግጥምሽ ይኖራል እንደ ድሮው እንደቀድሞው።
ይቀጥል እንጂ አያባራ ሕያው ግጥምሽ
ከቶ አያቁም፣ አይንጠፍ ውብ ብዕርሽ።   (19 May 2018)

የታቦት ቀን ትዝታ

ገና ድሮ በለጋው ወቅት በልጅነት
በጭፈራ ታጅቦ ሲጋዝ ታቦት
ለበዓል-ለዓመታዊ ንግሡት
ግሩም ድንቅ ነበር መመልከት።
ጊዜ የማይሽረው ሆኖ ዝክረ-ነገር
ቦታውን ይዞ ይኖራል በትዝታ ማህደር።

ቀሳውስቱ:- ታቦታቱን ተሸክመው
ከርቤ አንድደው
እጣን አጢሰው
በከፋይ በሐምራዊ በአልባሳት አጊጠው
ሲተሙ
ግርማ ሞገስ ተላብሰው ማየቱ
የመንፈስ ምልዓት ይሰጣል
ፍሥሐን ያላብሳል! ያንጻጽፋል።

ዘማሪዎች መቋሚያ ይዘው
በጸናጽል ቃጭል፣ በከበሮ ታጅበው
ድንቅ ዝማሬ በሽብሸባ ሲያስተጋቡ
ዕልልታው ይቀልጣል በአጀቡ።

ሆ እያለ
ሕዝቡ ሲተም፣ ሲጋፋ፣ ሲተራመስ
አማኑኤልን አልፎ ጥምቀተ-ባሕር ለመድረስ
ማየቱ ምንኛ ደስታን ይሰጣል
ትዝታው ሁልጊዜ ኑልቶ ይኖራል።   (20 May 2018)

ጨለማና ብርሃን

መከራና ሰቆቃ
ተስፋና እመቃ
ተጣርሶ ተደበላልቆ
ባንድ ላይ ተጨፍልቆ
ሞች ይሆን የሚጠራው?
ተበራይቶ የሚለየው፣
ሕይወት የሚከበረው፡፡

በሞት ደጃፍ ላይ ቆሞ
በጣረ-ሞት ተቆልምሞ
መቼ ይሆን የሚቆመው?
ሕይወት የማይቀነጠሰው፡፡

ኧረ መቼ ነው፣
በወገኑ እጅ የማይደማው
የማይወድመው የማይሞተው?

«ኤሎዬ ኤሎዬ ላማ ሰበቅታኒ» እንዳለው
አምላኩ እንዲታደገው
ደርሶ ሥጋውን እንዲያድነው
እንብል እንዬ ስለ ከቡር ሰው?   (21 May 2018)

የሃገር ትዝታ/ ስሜት

በጊዜ ርዝመት፤ በቦታ ርቀት
የማይወበይ፤ የማይገረጣ
የተወለዱበት፤ ያደጉበት
የኖሩበት፤ የሞቱበት
ረቂቅ ፍቅር ነው፤ ጥልቅ ስሜት
ሕያው ነው የሀገር ናፍቆት።

ከተማው ገጠሩ
ሜዳው ሸንተረሩ
ገደሉ ዱሩ
የቦረቁበት መንደሩ
መች ይረሳል ሐዘኑ ደስታውና ፍቅሩ?

የሁካታው የጸጥታው
የሐዘኑ የደስታው
የጋጋታው የእርጋታው
የፍንደቃው የእሮሮው
ተነባብሮ ተዋሕዶ ተጣምሮ
ይፈጥራል ግዙፍ ስሜት በአእምሮ።

ቅርብ መስሎ ሩቅ የሆነ
ከሐሳብ የማይፋቅ ያልመከነ
የሀገር ስሜት ጠሊቅ ነው
አንድ ቃል የማይፈታው
አንድ ሐረግ የማይገልጸው።

አረንጓዴ ልምላሜው
ተራራው ሸለቆው
አእዋፉ እንስሳቱ አራዊቱ
አዝርዕቱ ዕጽዋቱ

ያደጉበት መንደር
የዋሉበት ሰፈር
ዘመድ አዝማድ ጎረቤት
የተማሩበት ትምህርት ቤት
የተዝናኑበት የተደሰቱበት
በሐዘን የተኮማተሩበት
እንዳንዬም ቁም ስቅል ያዩበት
ረቂቅ ነው ጥልቅ ነው
የሀገር ስሜት።

የአንጸባራቂ ታሪክ ኩነት
የአባቶች፣ የእናቶች ጀግንነት
አርአያና ተምሳሌትነት
ጨዋነት ብልህነት
ይህ ሁሉ የሆነበት፣ የታየበት
እንድ ላይ ሲቀመር ነው
የሀገር ትዝታ የሚቀሰቅሰው
እንደ እሳት የሚነደው
የሚግለው ሐሳብን የሚያሞቀው።

ጥልቅ ነው ረቂቅ ነው
የማይወረዛ በጊዜ ርዝመት
የማይረሳ፣ የማይለካ በቦታ ርቀት
የሀገር ፍቅር የሀገር ስሜት።   (21 May 2018)

ግጥሞቼና ትዝታዎቼ   ፈቃዱ ፉላስ

የሃዋዬን እሳተ ገሞራ ማስታወሻ

የምድር ባሕርይ ውጥንቅጡ
ጥምዝምዙ ድጡ ማጡ
ስምጥ ሽለቆው፣ ሰማይ ጠቀስ አቀበቱ
የማያልቀው ቁልቁለቱ

ወንዝ መፍሰሻው፣ የውሃ ክምችቱ
የሜዳው የለምለም ዕፀዋቱ
የርሻ ማሳው፣ የማዕድን ክርሱ
የተስፋ ምንጯ፣ የሕይወት ፀንሱ

ደግሞም---

የእሳት ማህፀን
የሙቀት እቶን
የገሞራ ፍላት
የቅልጥ ትፋት
የሚንር እንደ ርችት
የሚጎን ወደ ሰማያት
ወርዶ ሲፈስ ሰው ለማጥፋት
ተምዘግዝጎ ተዝለግልጎ
ሰው ለማንደድ ሰው ለመግፋት

ዋ አንች ምድር ባለ ሁለት ራስ
ባለ ሁለት ምላስ
ባለ ሁለት ፊት
ባለ ጥንድ ባሕርያት
የልማትና የጥፋት!   (21 May 2018)

19

ባሕረ ግጥም

በግጥም ባሕር ገብቼ
እንዳልሰጥም ፈርቼ
እዋኛለሁ ተግቼ
በሐሳብ አቀዝፋለሁ ሞገዱን ገትቼ።
ኃያል ነው የግጥም መርከብ
ይወዘውዛል ማዕበል ለማርገብ።

ልክፍት ነው ወይስ አባዜ
ግጥም ሲወደድ እንዲህ ባንድ ጊዜ
እኔ ላልተወው ወይ እሱ ላይለቀኝ
ተያይዘናል አብረን ልንዋኝ
አብረን ልንናኝ
ሐረግ መዝገቤ ስንኝ ቋጥሬ
ቤት ለማነፅ የግጥም ፍሬ
እተጋለሁ እማስለሁ ደፍሬ።

የነበር አንቀላፍቶ ታምቆ
እንዳይወጣ ተቆልፎ ተደብቆ
ለዓመታት በብዕረ-ስንሰለት ታንቆ
ግና አሁን ማዕበል ፈጥሮ
ከውስጥ ስሜት ተፈንቅሎ ተውተርትሮ
ኃይለ-ቃል ፈጥሮ
የግጥም መከፈልቱን ሊወጣ
ጀምሯል ጠበሉን ሊያጠጣ
ድግሱን ሊያካፍል
ጠበል ጸዲቅ ቅመሱ ሊል
ቃለ ኃይል ፈጥሮ ነፍስ ዘርቶ
ተነስቷል ግጥም ሊሠራ በርትቶ።   (22 May 2018)

የጽጌረዳ አበባ ምሥጢር

የት ላይ ይሆን፤ የጽጌረዳ ውብቱ?
አእምሮን ሰርቆ፤ ልብን ማሸፈቱ።

ከሌሎች አበቦች ከሁሉም መላቁ
እንደ ወርቅ እንዳልማዝ እንደ ከበረ ዕንቁ

ቀለሙ ይሆን ወይ? ወይስ መዓዛው?
ስሜትን ማርኮ እርካታ የሚሰጠው
ያረፈ አካልን የሚቀሰቅሰው
በደስታ ፈንቅሎ የሚያነሳሳው።
ቀይ ቀለም ወይን ጠጅ ደግሞም ሰማያዊ
ቢጫ ተሸልሞ አሊያም ሐምራዊ
ጽጌረዳ አበባ፤ ነው ተአምራዊ።

ከሩቅ የሚስበው ማራኪ መዓዛው
የመውደድ የፍቅር መግለጫ ማብሰሪያው

በቀለማት ደምቆ አእምሮን ማስከሩ
መዓዛ አፍልቆ ልብን መበርበሩ
ፍቅርና መውደድን ባንድ ማጣመሩ
የጽጌረዳ አበባ ያ ነው ምሥጢሩ።
ተፈጥሮ ድንቅ ነው ምሥጢራት ያዘለ
ጠልቆ በተመስጦ በደንብ ላስተዋለ።

ጽጌረዳ አበባ የመውደድ አንደበት
የስሜት መግለጫ የፍቅር ምልክት።   (25 May 2018)

ከበሮ ሲመታ፣ በሃዘን በደስታ

በአንድ በኩል:-

ከበሮ ሲመታ፣ ዘፈኑ ሲደምቅ
ጭብጨባ ሲግል፣ ጭፈራ ሲሞቅ
እስክስታው ሲያምር፣ ልብን የሚሰርቅ
ያጥለቀልቃል የሰውን ስሜት
እንደ ማዕበል የደስታ ግፊት።

በሌላ በኩል:-

ከበሮ ሲመታ፣ ሊያሰማ ኧሮሮ
ሲቃ ሲተናነቅ፣ በሐዘን እንጉርጉሮ
ለቅሶና ሐዘን፣ ሰቆቃ ነግሦ
ሙሾ ሲወረድ፣ ሸርጥ ተለብሶ
ልብ ይሰበራል፣ ደስታ ደፍርሶ።

ምጭት:-

ደስታ ሊያሽንፍ ሐዘንን ሰብሮ
ተስፋ ሊነግሥ፣ ሀኬትን ቀብሮ
ያ ነው መጠይቁ መልስ የሚጠብቀው
የትኛው ይሆን ጎልቶ የሚወጣው? (27 May 2018)

ፀሐይ ሲዘንብ (የዘንድሮ ሙቀት)

ከረምቱን ሽሮ ፀደይ ብቅ ሲል
ፈገግ ያሰኛል፣ መንፈስ ያድሳል።

ለብሶ አረንጓዴ፣ ዛፉ ቁጥቋጦው
ደምቀው ፈክተው አበቦች በቀለም
ደኑን ሞልተው ቢራቢሮ፣ አዕዋፋት
ያረካል ማየት፣ ያድሳል አካል
አእምሮ ረከቶ፣ ድካም ይቀራል።

ግና--

ጸሐይ ተሾጉጦ በጎዋው ማህፀን በጣም በርቀት
ያ የከዋክብት ንጉሥ የጠፈር ትንግርት
ይተፋል እሳት፣ ያወርዳል መዓት
ዝንተ ዓለም የገሞራ ማዕበል
ዘላለም ነዲድ ሙቀት ነበልባል።

ግዙፍ ኃይል ሆኖ ሲረጭ ጨረሩን
በምድር ላይ ሲያዘንብ ሙቀት ወበቁን
ይለበልባል ትንፋሽ ያስይዛል
ገላን አቅልጦ በላብ ያጠምቃል።

ገና ከወዲህ ፀደይ ሳይወጣ
ዘንድሮ ጉድ ነው የአየሩ ጣጣ
የሚያቃጥል ነው በጋ ሳይመጣ።   (28 May 2018)

የወንድም (ዘነበ ፉላስ) ፍቅር

ዓመታት አልፈው ዘመን ሲተካ
ጥሎን ያልፋል የሕሳብ ዱካ
እንድንከተል መንገዱን ሳንስት
ሁሌ ስንደክም ሁሌም ስንዋትት
ቤት ለመመለስ ከተጓዝንበት
ጊዜ ይነጉዳል ፈጥሮ ትዝታ
የማይደበዝዝ ህያው ደስታ፡፡

ጓዴ ወንድሜ የምትኖር በልቤ
የማትለየኝ የምትኖር በሕሳቤ
ፋናዬ መንገዴ ለዝንተ ዓለም
መንፈስህ ይመራኛል
አይዞህ! ይለኛል ዛሬም፡፡

ያኔ የድሮው የልጅነትህ ፈገግታ
አሁንም ደማቅ ነው በሞት የማይገታ በጊዜ የማይፈታ፡፡

ካንድ ማህፀን ወጥተን፣ አንድ ላይ ኖረን
አንድ ልብ ይዘን፣ አንድ አካል ሆነን
ደስታና ሐዘን ባንድ ተጋርተን
አብረን ተምረን፣ አንድ ላይ አድገን
ኖረናል ሕይወት ሥቀን፣ ተጫውተን፣ ተደስተን፡፡

ተማምለን ነበር እንዳንለያይ
ቃል ገብተን ነበር በምድር በሰማይ
ጨለማ ሳይነግሥ ሳትሸሽ ፀሐይ
ደግሞም በጨረቃ በከዋክብት ብርሃን
ተመርተን ነበር እኛ የተስማማን

ዘመኑ አልፎ ባዲስ ሲተካ
ከቶ ላይመለስ ጨክኗል ለካ
እኛም ጊዜን ስናማ
ጊዜም እኛን ላይሰማ
እንፀናለን በያዝነው አላማ፨

ግና ምነዋ ጊዜ ቢቆም ቢቸከል?
እንዳይነቃነቅ እንዳይኮበልል
እንዳንለወጥ በጊዜ ግፊት በዘመን ርቀት
አቁመን ዕድሜን እዚያው ባለበት፨

ፍቅርህ ያረጠበኛል፣ እንደሚወርድ ዝናብ
ደምቆና ፈክቶ፣ ጎልቶ በምናብ
ያፀናኛል፣ ያፅናናኛል ዘውትር ትዝታህ
ዘልቆ ሕይወትን ያ ሩህሩህ ቃልህ
የኔና ያንተ የመንፈስ ውህደት
ፀንቶ ይኖራል እንደ አከሱም ሐውልት
ሳይነቃነቅ እንደ «ጂብራልታር» አለት፨   (28 May, 2018)

25

የተስፋ ጭላንጭል

ኢትዮጵያ--አንቺ ወላጅ እናት
የጀግኖች አምባ የታሪክ ቋት
የኩራት ምንጭ ኢትዮጵያ
የአእላፍ ዜኖች መመኪያ
ሙቀት የሚያፈልቅ ምቼ ዕቅፍሽ
ይጠብቃል፣ ይመክታል ብርቱ ክናድሽ።

ሩህሩህ ልብሽ የፍቅር ዓይንሽ
እናት ዓለም ምድረ አካልሽ
ተራሮችሽ አየር ጅረትሽ
የታሪክ እርከን የነድንቅነሽ
የሰው ዘር ምንጭ ተአምር ነሽ
የግዜር መዳና የፈጣሪ አንደበት
የምሥጢራት ሁሉ ነሽ መሠረት።

ጥንት እንደሆነው በረጅም ታሪክሽ
ዛሬም ትኖሪያለሽ በኩራትሽ ፀንተሽ
መከራን ድል ነስተሽ፣ ሕያው ትሆኛለሽ።

ግና ልጆችሽ ርስ በርስ ሲናከሱ
ጦር ሲመዙ ብረት ሲያነሱ
ኃይለኛው ደካማውን ሲቀማ፣ ሲገል
ከቀየው ሲገፋው ሲያፈናቅል
መስማት ያሳዝናል፣ ይከብዳል ማሰብ
ተንዣቦብሽ የስቃይ የሞት ድባብ።

እንዳያልፍ የለም ሁሉም ያልፋል

26

የተስፋ ብርሃን ደምቆ ታይቷል
የኢትዮጵያ ትንሣኤ ገና ይመጣል።

መልካሙ መጽሐፍ ቅዱስ እንዳለው
እንቺም በፈተና ሁሌም እንዳረግሽው
እጆችሽን ወደ እግዚአብሔር ዘርጊ
አይዞሽ ለሕዝብሽ አትስጊ
እንደ ትንግርተኛ «ፊኒክስ» አሞራ
ትነሻለሽ ከወደቅሽበት ትቢያ-አቢራ። (1 June ͺ 2018)

የሳይንቲስቱ ውሎ

የሳይንቲስቱ ውሎ አዳሩ
የት ይሆን ምህዳሩ
ኧረ የት ይሆን ሰፈሩ
ምን ይሆን ምሥጢሩ?

ውሎው የሐሳብ ጦር ሰፈር
የተሞላ በዳገት በሽንተረር
ሲለውም እንደ ሰፊ ባሕር
የራሱን ዓለም ፈጥሮ
የራሱን ልሳን ቀምሮ
ከተራው ሰው ተሰውሮ
ቋንቋው ልዩ አንደበቱ
ርቀቱ ምጥቀቱ ጥልቀቱ
የሚታወቅ ብቻ ለአባላቱ
ለዚያም ቢሆን ለጥቂቱ
በራሱ አውድማ ብቻ ላሉቱ፡፡

ሲጧጧፍ ውድድሩ ክርክሩ
ሲሰነጠቅ ሲታሽ ምርምሩ
እንደ ወርቅ አንጥረኛ
ሐሳብ ያቀልጣል ሳይተኛ፡፡

አንጥሮ ሊያወጣ ሐቅን
ሊያበስር ግኝትን
ዕንቆቅልሽን ሊፈታ
ከምስቅልቅሉ ገበታ
ለውሶ፥ አፍልቶ፥ ቀቅሎ
ደባልቆ፥ በትኖ፥ ቀጣጥሎ
አንፍሮ፥ አትንኖ፥ አጥልሎ

መትሮ፤ መዝኖ፤ ለከቶ
ጥቃቅኑን ለማየት አጉልቶ
በመነፅሩ ተመልክቶ
ይፈትሻል በሙከራ
መላ ምትን ሊያጣራ።

ዕውነቱን እንደ ሰብል ከምሮ
በሙከራ አበጥሮ
ለማውጣት አንጠርጥሮ
ይለፋል በሌሊት አድብቶ
ቀንም ቢሆን ተንከራቶ
ሐሳቡን በጥሞና አብራይቶ

እንደ እርጥብ ጨርቅ
አንጎሉን ሲጨምቅ
የውቀት ጎተራ ለማጨቅ
ይታትራል ከቶ ሳይወድቅ።

ልክ እንደ ታታሪ ገበሬ
ይጠብቃል ጥሩ ፍሬ
ለማሳየት ለታዳሚው
ለሳይንስ መንደር ነዋሪው።

ልፋቱ ድካሙ አልቆ
ለጊዜው ጉዞው ተጠናቆ
እፎይ ይላል ዘና ብሎ
ውጤቱን በፅሑፍ አዝሎ።

ምርቱ ለዳኞች ይቀርባል
ጥራቱን ለማብጠልጠል
ችሎቱ ግራ ቀኝ አይቶ
ይመረምራል ተግቶ
ማስረጃውን እንኮ አላምጦ
ውሳኔውን ይሰጣል በተመስጦ።

የብይን ቀን ሲደርስ
ሲቀርብ ሐተታ መልስ
ይለፍ ተብሎ ሲታወጅ
ሲባረክ በዳኞች እጅ
ይጥለቀለቃል ስሜት
ይሰፍናል ደስታ ኩራት።

የሳይንቲስት ውሎ አዳሩ
ያ ነው መቋጫው ሐረግ ክፉ። (02 June 2018)

የእፀዋት ጥቅም

መሬትን እንደጣራ ሸፍነው
ወይ ኪታች ምንጣፍ ሆነው
አሊያም ድኽው ሰማይ ታከው
ተንዞርገው ጥላ ሆነው
አየር ምገው አየር ተፍተው
ሆነው የሕይወት እስትንፋስ
ያድሳሉ የሰው አካል የሰው መንፈስ።

ብዙ ሥሪ ዕጽዋት
የሰው ልጆች ሃብት
በረከት ተዓምራት
የደስታ መሠረት ረከቦት
የሕይወት ምሥጢር በር
የአእላፍ ምሰሶ አውታር።

አረንጓዴ ለብሰው
መሬትን ሸፍነው
ሲታዩ ተውበው
በቀለማት ደምቀው
ያረካሉ ስሜት
ያድሳሉ ሕይወት።

ዛፉና ቁጥቋጦው
ደኑና ጫካው
ምድሪቱን ሸፍኖ
ዳር እስከዳር ሰፍኖ
አሽብርቆ አምሮ ሐረግ ሐመልማሉ
ዓይንን ይማርካል ሲታይ ጠንበለሉ።

ሰብልና አዝርእት
ሰጪ የእህል ምርት
ማገዶና አጥር
ማስጌጫ የመንደር
መገንቢያ ቤት መሥሪያ
የእንጨት መሣሪያ
የማይሆነው የለም
የእፀዋት ዓለም።

መድኃኒት ማስገኛ
የሕመም ማዳኛ
ውሕዶችን ፈጥሮ
ቀምሞ አጣምሮ
ታክሶል፣ ቶፖቲካን
ዲጀክሲን፣ ኳይናይን
እንዲሁም ሞርፊን
ልክ እንደ ፋብሪካ
ሲያዋሕድ ሲከካ
ያስደስታል ማየት
የተፈጥሮን ክህሎት
ድንቅ ነው ተአምሩ
ረቂቅ ነው ምሥጢሩ።   (05 June 2018)

በሁለት እግር የቆመ ስሜት

ተሰዶ ካገር ወጥቶ
ርቆ ተጉዞ ኑሮ መሥርቶ
ተምሮ ወይ ሥራ ሠርቶ
ትዳር ልጆች አፍርቶ
ቤተስኪያን መስጊድ ተክሎ
ካገሩ ሰው ተባብሮ
ሰፈር መንደር ፈጥሮ
ሕይወትን ይገፋል ጥሮ ግሮ
ግና ሁሌም በሐሳብ
ሀገር አይጠፋም ከልብ።

ያ የተወለዱበት መሬት
ዕትብት የተቀበረበት
ያደጉበት መንደር
የቦረቁበት ሰፈር
የደስታ የሐዘን ስሜት
የበዙበት የተፈራረቁበት
የማይገለጽ ፍቅር
የማይገሰስ ክብር
የታሪክ ተምሳሌት ባሕር
በልብ ዘላለም የሚኖር።

ወግ ባህሉ ጨዋታው
የማይጠፋ ትዝታው
አካሉ ውጭ ሐሳቡ ኢትዮጵያ
አንድ እግር እዚህ ሌላኛው እዚያ
አንድ ልብ እዚህ ሌላኛው ወዲያ
ክፉ ጠንካራ የማይበጠስ
ሁሌም ይኖራል የሀገር ፍቅር፤ የሀገር መንፈስ። (06 June 2018)

ቀንና ሌሊት

ምሥራቅ ተነስቶ ሥርቀተ ፀሐይ
ጀንበር ተጉዞ በሰፊው ሰማይ
ይዬዳል ምዕራብ ወደመጥለቂያው
እፎይ ለማለት ከቀኑ ጉዞው
አድማሱን ትቶ ከበስተኋላው፡፡

መዓልቱ አልፎ ሲተካ ሌሊት
ብርሃን ሲሸነፍ በጥቁር ምሽት
ፀሐይ ስትኃዝ በራን ለመዝጋት
ሰማይ ጥግ ደርሳ ምድር ዳርቻ
ትራሷ አድማስ መሰናበቻ
ቀይ ደም መስላ የእሳት አሎሎ
ለመሰናበት ከቀኗ ውሎ
ትበትናለች ወርቃማ ጨረር
ቀኑ ማለፉን ወዲያው ለማብሰር
ቃል ትገባለች ነገን ለማምጣት
ከምሥራቅ በኩል ካለው በርቀት
ሰማዩን ከፍታ ማልዳ በጥዋት፡፡

ሰውም ይነሳል ስትወጣ ጀንበር
የዕለት ውሎውን ቀኑን ሊጀምር
ቀጠሮ እንዳለው ከፀሐይ ጋር፡፡
ስትጠልቅ ደግሞ ይገባል ቤቱ
ጎኑን ሊያሳርፍ ለማታ እረፍቱ፡፡

ቋሚ-ዘላቂ የጊዜ ዑደት
ያፈራርቃል መዓልትና ሌት
ግና ውሱን ነው የሰው ልጅ ሕይወት
ጉዞ እስኪጨርስ እስኪሰናበት፡፡ (07 June 2018)

አይ የፍርድ ነገር

ዛሬ ጀግና ሲባል፣ ነገ ደግሞ ፈሪ
ፈሪው ጀግና ሲሆን በተዘዋዋሪ
የዛሬው ከሃዲ የነገው አርበኛ
እንደፈራጁ ዓይን፣ ሳይኖር መመዘኛ
የዛሬው ጨካኝ ሰው የነገው ገራገር
ይቀየራል ስሙ ቶሎ ባንዲት ጀንበር
የዛሬ ሩህሩህ ሰው ነገ ደግሞ ጨካኝ
ይበየንበታል ያለአንዳች ይግባኝ፡፡

ከቶስ ማን ይሆን ፈራጁ?
ንፁህ ብይን ያለው በእጁ.
ወይስ ይለያይ ይሆን ፍርድ?
ታይቶ በስሜት፣ በግል መንገድ
በጥላቻ ወይ በመውደድ
ይለያይ ይሆን እንደ አቋሙ?
ከፈራጁ መጣላቱ ወይ መጣጣሙ.

ምንለ እንድ መለኪያ ቢኖር?
መመዘኛው ቋሚና የሚከበር
እንደ እስስት የማይቀያየር
ወደ ላይ ጣት ሳይቀሰር
የነፋስን አቅጣጫ በማየት
ለመበየን፣ ፍርድ ለመስጠት፡፡

አይ የስሜት ፍርድ ነገር
እንደ ፈራጁ የሚቀያየር!   (09 June 2018)

ተፈራራቂ ስሜት (ፍልስፍና)

ልደትና ሞት ሐዘንና ደስታ
ሳቅና ለቅሶ፣ ጤናና በሽታ
ጨለማና ብርሃን፣ ዋይታና ፈገግታ
አዲሱና አሮጌው፣ የዛሬው የጥንቱ
ሁሌም ሲሳሳቡ፣ ሁሌም ሲጋተቱ
ይፈራረቃሉ በሰው ልጆች ሕይወት በሰው ልጆች ስሜት
አንዱ ሜዳ ሆኖ ሌላኛው ቁልቁለት ወይም አቀበት
ተስፋ የተሞላ፣ ወይ የሚቆርጥ አንጀት
ምን ይሆን ምሥጢሩ የሁሉቱ ክስተት?
መተያየታቸው ተፋጠው በርቀት
መተሳሠራቸው እንዳንዴም በቅርበት
አንደኛው ይስባል ወደ ራሱ አቅጣጫ
ሌላውም ይጥራል እርሱ እንዲሆን ምርጫ።

አንደኛው ከሌላው ከቶ አይለይም
አንደኛው ከሌላ ሌላኛው አይኖርም።

ስሜት ሲፈራረቅ፣ ተቃራኒ ዓለም
ጉትቻው፣ ስበቱ ይኖራል ዘላለም።   (10 June 2018)

ድልድዩ ሲቋረጥ (ፍልስፍና)

ጊዜ ያልፋል ዘመን ይተካል
አክናፍ እንዳለው ሁሉ ይበራል
ላይመለስ ወደፊት ይነጉዳል
አንዳንዴም የቆመ ይመስላል፡፡

ይፈሳል ጊዜ እንደ ጅረት
እንደ ደራሽ ውሃ ሙላት
ሲለው፣ ሰው ለመውሰድ ድንገት
እንደ መቅሰፍት፣ መልአከ ሞት

ደግሞም፡-
ብልጭ ድርግም እንደ ብራቅ
ምድር ሰማይን ለመነቅነቅ
ሐዘን ስቆቃን ለማድረቅ
ጎርባጣ ሕይወትን ለማረቅ
የሀሴት ብርሃን ለመፈንጠቅ
የጎበጠውን ለማቃናት
ጨለማውን ለማብራት
እንደ ሰማይ ኮከብ ሲወረወር
በጯራው ተስፉን ለማብሰር
ትካዜ መከራን ሊሰብር
ጊዜ ይጥራል ደስታ ሊፈጥር፡፡

አይቀድሙት ወይ ከኋላው አይከተሉት
ይንዛሉ አብረው በጊዜ ቅፅበት
ተስፋና ትዝታን ብቻ ለማየት
ጊዜ ሲያልፍ ሲመጣ ወደፊት፡፡

በሌላ ገጹ ጊዜ ያዞግማል
የተረገመ፣ የተወገዘ ይመስል
እንዳይሄድ ነቅንቅ እንዳይል
የተፈረደበት ይመስል
ማለቂያ መዝጊያ የሌለው ጊዜ
ይዞታል የማይልቅ የመንፏቀቅ አባዜ።

በረጅም የሕይወት ጉዞ ውስጥ
ዕድሜ ሲገፋ፣ ድንበር ሲቃረጥ
ቆም ይባላል በጥሞና ለማሰብ
ነገር ሁሉ ሲነባበር ሲደራረብ
የክንውን ውጤትን ለማጤን
መነሻ መዳረሻውን ለመመዘን
ተመልሶ በዓይን ኃሊና ሲቃኝ
የተሟላ እርካታ ላይገኝ
ያልተሠራው ሁሉ ሲኰለኰል
ከአንግዲህስ ምን ቀረኝ ሲባል

እያንዳንዱ የዕድሜ እርከን
የልጅነት ወጣትነት ዘመን
የጎልማሳነት አዛውንትነት
ሲታይ በትዝታ መስተዋት
አለው የራሱ ድምቀት
የፈተና የውድቀት ወይ የስኬት።

ድልድዮችን አቋርጦ ተሻግሮ
ይኖራል ሰው ተስፋ ቋጥሮ። (12 June 2018)

የዝምታ ትርጉም (ፍልስፍና)

የጸጥታ፣ የዝምታ መልእክቱ
ምን ይሆን እንድምታው ስሜቱ?
ለካስ ሳይናፉ መናገር
በዝምታ ሐሳብን መሰደር
ይቻላል በነገር መስማማት
ወይ ጸጥ ብሎ ያለመስማማት
ያ ይሆን የዝምታ መልእክት?

አሊያም ስሜትን አድብቶ
ከችኮላ ከጥላቻ ርቆ ወጥቶ
ጊዜ ወስዶ ግራ ቀኝ አይቶ
ለመናገር ይሆን ዘግይቶ?

የጥንቱ የአበው ብሂል
«ዝምታ ወርቅ ነው» እንደሚል
ወይስ እንደ ሌላው አባባል
«ካለመናገር ደጃዝማችነት ይቀራል»?

ከሁለቱ የሚሻለው የቱ ይሆን
«ደጃዝማች» ወይስ «ወርቅ» መሆን?   (13 June 2018)

ጎስኛነት (የፖለቲካ አስተያየት)

ይህ የጎሰኛነት መቅሰፍት
ስብእናን የሚያዋርድ መዓት
ሰውን ከሰውነቱ አውጥቶ
በጎሳ ሳጥን ውስጥ ከቶ
ይዶለዋል ሰው መሆኑን ረስቶ።

ደግሞም ይሉታል ብሄር-ብሄረሰብ
ተውሶ ከምሥራቅ ወይ ደቡብ
ውዲቷ ኢትዮጵያን ሳያገናዝብ
የግል መብት ነጻነት ተረስቶ
በቡድን ትርጉም ተሰልቶ
ተተርጉሞ፣ ተቆርጦ፣ ተሾልቶ
ምን ሊጠቅመው ለገበሬው
ለዚያ ታታሪ ምስኪን ድሃው
በከተማ ተግቶ ለሚዳክረው
ከቶ ምን ሊረባው ምን ሊጠቅመው
ይህ የጎሳ መለያው፣ መጠሪያው።

ጎሰኛነት ጽኑ ህመም ነው
ምናልባት ጊዜ የሚሽረው
አሜን እንበል እስከዚያው።   (14 June 2018)

ግጥሞቼና ትዝታዎቼ   ፈቃዱ ፉላስ

የምዕራብ ሃገሮች በጋና ክረምት ሹዋሹዋይ

አባ እሳት፣ አባ አንፍር
አባ ቃጠሎ፣ አባ ጨረር
አባ ቀቅል፣ አባ አንጨርጭር
ሰውን ሊያቀልጥ ሰው ሊመትር
ሊቀጣው በሙቀት በትር
በጋ አይተው በጋ አይምር፡፡

ገላን ገልጦ ሙቀት ንቆ
በጋን ያልፉል ባጭር ታጥቆ፡፡

ታዲያ ያ ሁሉ አልቆ
ክረምት ይመጣል ገዝፎ
በመሃል ፀደይን ፍቆ፣ ገፎ፡፡

ነጭ ምንጣፍ ዳር እስከ ዳር
መሬት ሲለብስ በረድ ክምር
ሊያቀዘቅዝ ሊያኮማትር
ቆዳ አልቆ፣ ጠልቆ ደም ሥር
ብርድ ይገባል ሊሰረስር፡፡

ደራርቦ ልብስ፣ ተሸፋፍኖ
ከውስጥም እንዲሁ ተጀቡኖ
ራስ፣ ጆሮ ተጠምጥሞ ተሸፍኖ

ጥርስ ያፋጭል ጆሮ ያቀላል
እንደ ዛር ያንዘፈዝፋል
«የሙቀት ያለህ» ያስኛል፡፡

41

ክረምት ያልፋል ብርዱን ውጦ
ለመጪው ዓመት ቀን ቆርጦ።
ይመጣል ቢጋ በተራው
በወላፈን ሰውን ሊቀጣው።

የሰውም ሕይወት አንዲሁ ነው
ተለዋውጦ ተፈራርቆ የሚመጣው! (15 June 2018)

ሞትና ሕይወት

ሕይወትና ሞት፣ የት ላይ ነው ድንበሩ?
የእስትንፋስ ማለቂያው ምሥጢሩ?
ልብን አተራምሶ፣ እንዳይሠራ ኢድክሞ
አንጎልን አናውጦ፣ አስለምልሞ
አካልን አ'ዝሎ እንዳይሠራ አቁሞ
ያኔ ነው መጣሁ የሚል
ጣረ ሞት ደረስሁ የሚል
ሊሟገት ከሕይወት ጋር
ነፍስን ሊያንሳፍፍ ባየር
በድን አካልን ሊያስቀር

ነፍስም ይታገላል በድፍረት
ሞትን ድል ለመንሳት
ኃይሉን ሰብስቦ ለማሸነፍ
ላለመውደቅ ላለማረፍ።
ይህ ሞት የሚባል ነገር
ነፍስ የሚሉት ነገር
መንፈስ የሚባል ነገር
የሚነገር በቁሚው ሰው
ምን ይሆን መገለጫው?
ከቶ የት ነው መግቢያ መውጫው?
የማይታይ የማይነበብ
ግን የሚኖር በሐሳብ
ያ ደብዛዛ መስመር
የማይዳሰስ ድንበር
ተነግሮ ብቻ በአንደበት
ይለያል ሞትን ከሕይወት። (16 June 2018)

ስለ ሙዚቃ/ ዘፈን

ረቂቅ ቋንቋ ነው፣ ሙዚቃ ዘፈን
የሚቀሰቅስ ጠልቆ ስሜትን
ደስታ፣ ሐዘንን እንዲሁም ፍቅርን
ይናገራልም ሆኖ ቃል አልባ
ሙዚቃ ልብ ውስጥ ሰርጾ እየገባ።

ሐሳብ ስሜትን ይዞ ይነጉዳል
ዘፈን ሲሰማ ልብ ይሽፍታል
ለቅሶና ደስታ ይቀላቅላል
ያውጃል መውደድ፣ ያበሳል ፍቅር
ግፉ ሲለውም ዘልቆ እስከዳር
ክንፍ አስወጥቶ ይስቅላል ባየር።

በቃል ተውቦ፣ በዜማ ደምቆ
አእምሮን ማርኮ፣ ስሜትን አንቆ
ያፍከነክናል፣ ያስጨፍራልም
ቀጾና ፈጥሮ የራሱን ዓለም።

የፍቅር ውበት፣ የሰቆቃ ወላፈን
የእምነት ጽናት፣ የተስፋ ውጋጋን
ረቂቁ ሙዚቃ፣ ማህደረ ልሳን
ይናገራል ስሜትን፣ ያስተጋባል ሐዘን። (17 June 2018)

ፍቅር ምንድነው?

ምንድነው መውደድ? ምን ይሆን ፍቅር?
ይኖረው ይሆን መጋቢያ መውጫ በር?
ቶሎ ጀምሮ በጊዜ የሚዳብር
የሚቆይ ይሆን እስከ መቃብር?
ወይስ ያለው ነው የራሱ እድሜ
ቀስ ብሎ ሳስቶ ያለው ፍጻሜ?
የሚጠወልግ ከስሞ የሚቀር
በጊዜ ርዝመት የማይደርስ ከዳር?

የቁመናና የአእምሮ ውበት
ጥምሩ አንድ ላይ ይፈጥራል ስሜት
ያመጣል ስበት ልክ እንደ ማግኔት
ይፈጥራል ንዝረት፣ ያስነሳል ግለት።

ቀላል ነው ማየት ቁመና አካልን
ግና ይከብዳል ማወቅ ጠባይን
ቁንጅና ከባሕርይ ካልተሳሰረ
ፍቅር አይኖርም ካልተጣመረ።

የአእምሮና የጠባይ ብስለት
በልጦ ይወጣል ከአካል ውበት
ሲመጣጠን ነው የሁለቱ ሚዛን
ፍቅር የሚዘልቅ ለብዙ ዘመን። (17 June 2018)

መደመር (የለውጥ ነፋስ)

መደመር፣ መቀነስ፣ ማባዛት፣ ማካፈል
አራቱ መደቦች የቀመር ማዕከል
መደመር ይመጣል ቀድሞ ከሌሎቹ
ስሌት እንዲሳካ ጉዞ እንዲሆን ምቹ
ይኸው በለጠና በሂሳብ ዓለም
ሁሉን አያይዞ መክፈል እንዲከስም
ተነሳ በፍጥነት ዐቢይ «ደምሬ»
ችግር ከፍፍልን ሊያስገባ ከጎሬ
ሊቀር ነው መክፈል፣ ሊቀር ነው ማጣፋት
ከአራት መደብ አልፎ በትልቁ መሬት
ይቅናው፣ ይቅናን ድምሩ ይሳካ
አሜን እንበልለት እንዳይገዋመው ሳንካ። (22 June 2018)

ህከምና በግጥም ዓይን

አካል ሲቃወስ፣ ሲዛባ አእምሮ
በሽታ ሲይዝ፣ ህመም ጠንክሮ
ህከምና-መድኃኒት ይደርሳል ቶሎ፣ ይመጣል በሮ።

ሞያው ከቡር ነው የተቀደሰ
ጥበብ፣ ርህራሄ የተላበሰ
ትጋት፣ ሥነ ምግባር ባንድ ያጣመረ
ከሰው ሕይወት ጋር የተሳሰረ።

አካልን ዳብሶ፣ ታሪክ አጥንቶ
ትንፋሽ አድምጦ፣ ምስሎችን አይቶ
ምልክቶችን አይቶና አገናዝቦ
ያቀናጀዋል ሳይንስ አንግቦ።
ፈሳሽ መርምሮ፣ ደጋሞም ፈትሾ
ፈልፍሎ ያወጣል የህመም መነሾ።

አካል ውስጥ ገብቶ፣ ቆርጦ ቀጥሎ
የተዛባውን አቅንቶ አስተካክሎ
አሊያም በመድኃኒት ጉትቶና አርሞ
ያስታግሰዋል እንዳይብስ ደግሞ።
ጥበቡ ድንቅ ነው፣ ያረዘማል ሕይወት
ሁሌም ይተጋል ጤናን ለማምጣት
ሆኖም አይቀርም አንድ ቀን ማለፍ፣ አንድ ቀን መሞት

47

እናም፦
ጊዜው ሲመጣ አካል ሲደክም
አአምሮ እንዲሁ ባከኖ ሲስለመለም
ይፈትሿል ጥራት የሕይወትን ትርጉም

ይሻላል ማለፍ ሳይሰቃዩ
አንጎል ሳይስቱ፣ ዘመድ እያዩ
ቤተሰብ ከቦ እየጸለዩ። (24 June 2018)

ቂም ነገርና ቀልድ

ተፈራራቂ ቂም ነገር ወይ ቀልድ
ሁልጊዜ ሲታይ ባንድ ወጥ መንገድ
አንዱን ያስቃል ሌላውን ሲያነድ፡፡
ስሜት ሲጎዳ ወይም ሲያደስት
ይገርማል በጣም የሁለቱም መልእክት፡፡

ምፀት ወይ ስላቅ የቀልድ ምሰሶ
ቂም ነገር አዝሎ ጎሊናን ዳሶ
በምፀት-በቀልድ ሐሳብ ሲነገር
ለሚያጤነው ሰው ይገባል ምሥጢር
ነጭ ወይ ጥቁር ብቻ ለሚያያው
ይዘት ሐሳቡን ጠልቆ ካላየው
ያለመግባባት ችግር ይፈጥራል
በግልፅ አእምሮ ማየት ይበጃል፡፡   (04 July 2018)

ተስፋ

እንዴት ይሆን ያለ ተስፋ ሰው የሚኖር
ያለ ራዕይ ያለ ፍቅር
ኧረ ምን ይሆን የሕይወት ምሥጢር
ትርጉሙስ ምንድነው የመኖር?

ከሆነ የኍላ ጉዞ ሁሌ ለማላዘን
የዛሬን ችግር ላይፈታ የቆየ ቁስልን ላያድን
ምን ሊበጅ ካልገፋፋ ጨለማና ሐዘንን
ግና ወደኋላ ማየት መመልከት
ካልተገኘበት ትምህርት
እንዲያው ብቻ ለመቆጨት
ወይ ለመበቀል ለመጠፋፋት
ከሆነስ ይቅር ይረሳ ይሙት
ዳግም እንዳይነሳ እንዳያጠፋ ሕይወት፡፡

ምን እርባና ምን ፋይዳ ሊኖረው
ይሆናል አዙሪት እንደሚኾር እንደሚሽከረከረው
ወደ ጀመረበት ሊመልሰው
ሰቆቃን ሐዘንን ለመመለስ
ጦርነት ዕልቂትን ለማንገሥ

ታዲያ ለዚህ ሁሉ
ተስፋ ይሁን መልሱ
ጨለማ ይመለስ ወደ ከርሱ
ብሩህ ይሁን አድማሱ፡፡   (15 July 2018)

የኢትዮጵያ ትንሣኤ

መንግሥት ጥሎ፣ መንግሥት ተክሎ
የበፊቱን አውግዞ፣ አጣጥሎ
ቃል ይገባል ፍትህ ለማንገሥ
ሕዝብ ለማንሳት፣ ታሪክ ለማደስ።

ግና፡-
ግፍ ግፍን ወልዶ
ዓመጽ ዓመጽን ፈጥሮ
ዓመታት አሳብሮ፣ ዘመናት ተሻግሮ
ሕይወት ቀጥፎ መንፈስ ሰብሮ
ወኔ ሰልቦ፣ ሃሞት አፍሶ
ፍቅር አምክኖ፣ ተስፋ ደርምሶ
ሕዝብ ይገፋል፣ ይበትናል
ያናቁራል ያጋጫል፣ ያሳድዳል።

ኗሊናን ከድቶ፣ ታሪክ ሸሮ
በዘር ከፋፍሎ፣ ሀገር ቀብሮ
ታዲያ ዛሬ ያ ሁሉ ሲረሳ
የኢትዮጵያ ስም በኩራት ሲነሳ
ምንኛ ደስ ይላል፣ ምንኛስ መንፈስ ያድሳል
የለውጡ ማዕበል ተስፋን ይዘራል
የኢትዮጵያን ትንሣኤ ያቀርባል፣ ያፋጥናል። (25 July 2018)

ቀስተ ደመና – ኢትዮጵያ

ቀስተ ደመና በሰማይ ላይ
የደጋን ቅርጽ ይዞ በቀለም ኅብር ሲታይ
ሲደምቅ ሲኳላ ባረንዷዬ ቢጫ ቀይ
ሀገርን ሊያስታውስ የባንዲራን ቀለም
ያበስራል ያቺን ውብ እናት ዓለም።

ሳይዛነፍ ከሃዲዱ፣ ተነስቷል ፈጣን ባቡር
ጉዞ ጀምሯል ወደ ተስፉ ምድር።

ምንም እንኳን—
ጋሬጣው ሰንኮፉ ቢደረደር
እንቅፋት ሆኖ ለውጡን ሊሽር

ግና ይወጣል ከዓመፅ መስመር
ከስቃይ ከእንግልት ባሻገር
የኢትዮጵያን ታሪክ ሊዘክር
ተነስቷል ከዳር እስከዳር።

በቀስተ ደመና ተመስሎ
ካጽናፍ አጽናፍ ተደላድሎ
ይታያል በሰማይ ተንጣሎ።

እንች ምሥጢረኛ ሀገር
ትንግርታዊ የታሪክ ባሕር
የኩሩ ሕዝብ ምድር
የሞላብሽ ጀግና ደፋር
የጥንታዊ ዕውቀት በር
በተራራ በሽለቆ ያጌጥሽ
በአረንጓዴ ልምላሜ የተዋብሽ

በቀስተ ደመና የተሸለምሽ
ይውለበለባል ባንዲራሽ
ሰማይ ምድሩን ገና ያጌጣል
ታሪከ፣ ዝናሽ ይዘከራል።

ቀስተ ደመናሽ በሰማይ ያብራ
ሕዝብሽ በባንዲራሽ ይኩራ
ለዘላለም ኑሪ ኢትዮጵያ
ሁኚ የልጆችሽ መኩሪያ።   (27 July 2018)

የሃገር ፍቅር

አይገልጹት ነገር አይናገሩት
በበቂ አይጽፉት በጅ አይዳስሱት
ረቂቅ ነው ጠሊቅ አዝለው እሚኖሩት
ብቻ የሚገኝ በደም በስሜት።

ልክፍት አይሉት ወይም በሽታ
የሕዝብ ፍቅር የሀገር ትዝታ
የሚፈነቅል በታላቅ ደስታ
ሐዘንም ሃሴትም ተቀላቅሎበት
ይኖራል ጠልቆ፣ ሰርጾ በሕይወት።

ቃል የማይፈታው ዘልቆ ከሥሩ
ከቶ ምን ይሆን ጥልቅ ምሥጢሩ
የዕንቆቅልሹ ማረፊያ ምህዳሩ
ኧረ የት ይሆን ሰፈር መንደሩ
የኢትዮጵያ ፍቅር የት ነው ድንበሩ?

ርቆ የሚቀርብ ቀርቦ የሚርቅ
ዘመን ሳይሸረው እንደ ደማቅ ወርቅ
ጠልቆ የሚኖር በልብ በሐሳብ
የማይጠወልግ ሁሌም የሚያብብ
ልክፍት ይሆን፣ ወይ ሌላ ነገር
ይህ ደማቅ ስሜት፣ የሀገር ፍቅር
ከቶም ሳይወበይ ዘላለም ይኑር። (30 July 2018)

ጎሰኝነት

ገና ድሮ የልጅነት፣ የጨርቃነት
ንጹሕ ስሜት የነገሠበት
አእምሮ ያልተበከለበት
ይናፍቃል ያ ጊዜ ያ ዘመን
ሁሉም የሚታይበት እንደ ወገን።

ምነው ያ ስሜት ባያድፍ ባይጨቀይ
በጎሰኝነት ፀያፍ ብካይ
ንጹሕ መንፈስ ያልተበከለ
ሁልጊዜ ህያው ቢሆን ምናለ?

ገና ጊዜ ተቀይሮ ተበላሽቶ
ሰውነት በጎሳ ሳጥን ተከቶ
ገና ሲወለድ ሲድህ ሲያድግ
መርጦ ሳይሆን ተሰብኮ በግድ
በውልደቱ የዘር ማህተብ አስሮ
በጎሳ ታትሞ፣ ሰውነቱ ተሰውሮ
ምንኛ ክፋት ነው አስነዋሪ
የሚያስወጣ ከሰውነት ባህሪ።

መቼም ተስፋ አይሞትም
ሰውነት ገዝፎ መውጣቱ አይቀርም።። (01 August 2018)

የወጣትነት ዘመን

ይመስል ነበር ሁሌም የሚኖር
የወጣትነት ጠሊቅ ምሥጢር
ብርቱ አካል፣ ትኩስ አእምሮ
የሚጋዝ፣ የሚዘልቅ ጊዜን ሽሮ
ዕድሜን ጥሎ አሽቀንጥሮ

የወጣትነት ትኩሱ ኃይል
የሚጋጓ የሚቸኩል
ጊዜን ለመምታት ድል
በፀሓይ ብርሃን ድምቀት
በጨረቃ ፀዳል፣ ፍካት
ገና ሳይጨልም ሕይወት
መዓልት ሳይከስም ሳይመጣ ጽልመት
ይቀርባል ከማዕዱ ድግስ
መዝጊያ መከፈልቱን ሊቋደስ።

ይመስል ነበር ተቀድቶ ያማያልቅ
የወጣትነት ዕድሜ የሚዘልቅ
በጥልቅ ባሕር ተከሎ መልሕቅ
ሲያጠምድ ዕውቀት
ሲያድን ትምህርት።

ያ ጊዜ የአፍላ ሕይወት
ለካስ ያልፋል በፍጥነት
ይደክማል አእምሮና ሰውነት
ላይመለስ እንደቀድሞው
እንደ ጥንቱ እንደነበረው።

እፎይ ይላል አካል
ያልቃል የሕይወት ገድል
ለመጪው ትውልድ ያውጃል
ችቦውን ተረከቡ ይላል። (12 August, 2018)

ይብላኝለት ለሻሽመኔ

ታየ ዛሬ ባደባባይ
በብርሃን በጠራ ሰማይ
ሰው ከቦ ጥሎ ግዳይ።

የራሱን አምሳል የአካሉን ከፋይ
ዘቅዝቆ ሰቅሎ ስልክ እንጨት ላይ
የት ይሆን ገደቡ፤ ማቆሚያው ድንበሩ
የጭካኔ ልኩ፤ የሰቆቃ ዳሩ
ለካስ ይሰጥማል ቅጥ አጥቶ
ወደ ድቅድቅ ጨለማ ገብቶ
እንዲያ ዘቅጦ፤ እንዲያ በከቶ
ዓመፅ አርግዞ ጭካኔ ወልዶ
ኧረ ምን ጉድ ነው ምንኛ መርዶ።

ሲአል ታየ በምድር ላይ
በሻሽመኔ አደባባይ
ቀራንዮ አገኘች አቻ
ኧረ ጉድ ነው ባሰ ብቻ
ወደ ሰማይ አቅንቶ
«ኤሎሄ ኤሎሄ ላማ ሰበቅታኒ» እንዳይል
ፈጣሪውን ተቀበለኝ እንዳይል
ዘቅዝቆ እንዲያ ማድረግ
ሻረው የሞትን መጨረሻ ወግ።

ይብላኝ ላንቺ እኔስ መጥኔ
ለአደባባይሽ ለሻሽመኔ
ነፍስ ይማር ለወንድሜ ለወገኔ። (13 August 2018)

የባህል መድኃኒት በግጥም መልክ

የአበው የእመው ክህሎት
ለትውልድ የሚሄድ ትውፊት
ጤቃሚ የሃገር፥ የወገን ቅሪት
የዘመናዊ ህክምና መሠረት
ሀገር-በቀል ባህላዊ መድኃኒት።

ታክሶል፥ ቪንክሪስቲን፥ ቆኃቲካን
ያዘጋሉ ሂደተ-ካንሰርን።
ያስተውሷል አጅሬ ዲጆክሲንን
ልብ ሲውተፈተፍ - ሲያበዛ ቅጥ ያጣ ንዝረትን
ከተፍ ይላል ታዋቂው ሞርፊን
ሊያረግብ የህመም ሥቃይን
ኧረ ስንቱ ተነግሮ ተተርኮ
ተፈጥሮ የሚሰጠን ባርኮ።

ፈጥኖ ደራሽ ድንገተኛ
ሆድ ቁርጠትን ሊያስተኛ
የባሕር ዛፍ ቅጠል እንፋሎት
ባፍንጫ ሲሰቡት ሲታጠኑት
ይከፍታል መተንፈሻ ሳንባን
የአየር መሳቢያ ቱቦን
ሊታደግ ሳል፥ ጉንፋንን።

ይደግ ይመንደግ የባሕል መድኃኒት
ነውና ባህላችን ጥንታዊ ትውፊት። (07 Sept 2018)

ዕንቁጣጣሽ

ዕንቁጣጣሽ ዐዉደ ዓመት
የብሩህ ዘመን ብሥራት
የአሮጌ ዓመት ማብቂያ
የአዲስ ዘመን ማብሰሪያ
የዝናም ወራት ማክተሚያ
የአበቦች መፍኪያ መታያ።
አደይ አበባ አንግባ
በቀለማት፣ በዘፈን ታጅባ
ብቅ አለች ዕንቁጣጣሽ
ደስታ ሰጪ፣ መንፈስ አዳሽ።

የበሬና የበጉ ጋጋታ-ቱማታ
የዶሮው ማስካካት እሪታ
የልጆች፣ የአዋቂዎች ጫጫታ
ትዕይንት ነው የገበያው ሁካታ።
አዲስ ዓመት ዕንቁጣጣሽ
ተኳኩለሽ እንኳን መጣሽ።

ቤተሰብ፣ ዘመድ አዝማድ
ይቋደሳል ከአንድ ማዕድ።
የቤት ወለል አምሮ በቄጠማ
በደማቁ በዓል ዋዜማ
ድፎ ዳቦ፣ አርኪ ጠላው
አረቄው፣ ወጡ፣ እንጀራው
ቤቱን ሲያዉድ ድንቅ መዓዛው
ዘፉን ሲቃልጥ በኢዮሃ አበባዬ
ይባላል መስከረም ጠባዬ። (09 Sept 2018–ጳጉሜን 4, 2010)

የቡራዩ መዓት

ትርምሱ፣ ውጥንቅጡ፣ ዕልቂቱ
ስደት፣ እንግልት፣ ጣረ ሞቱ
ሕዝብ በጅምላ የሚሞትበቱ
እንደከብት የሚታረድበቱ
እኮ ምን ይሆን ምክንያቱ?
መነሻው መሠረቱ?
ሰውን የሚያስወጣው ከሰውነቱ።

እስኪ ተጠየቂ አንች ቡራዮ?
መልስ ካለው ጉዳዩ፣ ግዳዩ
ለካስ የሰው ጭካኔ ወሰን የለው
ሞትም እኮ ወግ ሥርዓት አለው
እንዴት አካል ተቆርጦ ተበጣጥሶ
የግዜር መቅደስ በአብሪት ተጥሶ
ይጣላል እንደከብት በየስርቻው
ምንም ዋጋ እንደሌለው?

ህጻናት አዛውንት ደካሞች
መከታ ያጡ ጉብል ሴቶች
የማይመርጥ ጨካኝ መንፈስ
ይውረድ አዘቅት፣ እንጦርጦስ
ዳግም ቡራዮ እንዳይመለስ። (22 Sept 2018)

የድሮ—የእህቶቼን ሠርግ ሳስታውስ የተጻፈ

የሠርግ ድግስ ዝግጁቱ
ሳይረፍድ ገና በጥዋቱ
ገና ሲቀር ሳምንታት ወራቱ
ይጀመራል ማድረቅ ጌሾ
የመጥመቂያው መነሾ
ሊታጨቅ በሙቀጫ ቁት
ሊወርድበት የዘነዛ ምት
ሊደለቅ ሊጎን እንደ ዱቄት
የሙቀጫው ወገብ ዳሌም
በግር እስር፣ በእጅ ጥምጥም
ይያዛል ተደርጎ ግ'ጥም
እንዳይል ውልፍ፣ ዘለም
በሁለት ሦስት ፈረቃ
ሳይሰነጠር ከቶ ሳይነቃ
ችሎ የዘነዛን ምትና ሰቆቃ
ጭብጨባው ይቀልጣል
በርታ ጎበዝ ይባላል
ዱቄት ይበተናል ወደ አየር
አፍንጫ ትንፋሽን ለማፈን።።
ይህ ሁሉ ጠላ ለመሆን
ሊገባ ወደ እንስራ ወደ ጋን
ሊለቆጥ ከአሻሮ-እንኩሮ ጋር
ሰነባብቶ ሲበስል ይወደሳል
ኮሳል ያለ «የድሮ ዓይን» ይባላል።።   (04 Nov 2018)

የምድጃ እሳት ዳር ጨዋታ

ተጸዳድቶ «ደጅ» ተወጥቶ
ሁሉም ከትቶ፣ ከቤት ገብቶ
ቀኑ መሽቶ፣ በር ተዘግቶ
አካል ያርፋል ዘና ብሎ
የቀን ኮተት ሐሳብ ጥሎ።

በምድጃው ሲነድ ከሰል
ሲለቅ ሙቀት ፍሙ ሲግል
ቤተ - ሰቡ ዙሪያው ከቦት
ይጀምራል የወግ ሥርዓት
ዕንቆቅልሽ ተረት ተረት።

ሲንተከተክ ቡናው ፈልቶ
ጎረቤቱ ይገናኛል ተጠራርቶ።
ይደምቃል ቀልዱ፣ ጨዋታው
ቁም ነገሩ - ሐሜታው-አሉባልታው።

የምድጃው የእሳት ዙሪያው
የምሽቱ የቀን መዝጊያው
እንዲያ ነበር መዝናኛው።   (05 Nov 2018)

ዑደተ ጊዜ

ቀኑ ይነጋል ቀኑ ይመሻል
ፀሓይ ይጠልቃል፤ ምሽት ይነግሣል
ብርሃንና ጽልመት ይፈራረቃል።
አንዱ ወር አልቆ ሌላው ይተካል
በጊዜ ገመድ ይተሳሠራል
ዓመቱ አልቆ መጪው ብቅ ይላል።

ዘንድሮ ካምና ችበውን ወስዶ
ይነጉዳል ዘመን ሳይወድ ተገዶ።
በጋው አልቆ ክረምት ይተካል
ዛሬ ይሞቃል ነገ ይበርዳል
በዑደት ሥርዓት - ደንብ ይፈራረቃል።
በልግና ፀደይ ድልድይ ይሆናል
ሁለቱን ጽንፎች ያስተሳስራል
ወደ ተስፋ ዓለም ያሸጋግራል።

እንደ አየር ንብረት፤ በሽታ አባዜ
የሰውም ስሜት ልክ እንደጊዜ
ተጠልቆ እንዳይወድቅ በውዝዋዜ
ንጹሕ ሒሊናን በጥብቅ ጨብጦ
መኖር ግድ ይላል ዕውነትን መርጦ።   (13 Nov 2018)

ስሜት

ነዲድ ነው ነበልባል ስሜት
የልብ ቤተ - መቅደስ ታቦት
ደማቅም ነው እንደ ከዋክብት።

በሰማይ ጣሪያ እንደ አሸዋ ፈሶ
ያበራል ጎዋውን ጨለማን ደምሶ።

ሲለው ይሆናል ነጭ ምንጣፍ
ደማቅ ሥጋጃ በደመና ደጃፍ
በፀሓይ ጸዳል ደምቆ አሽብርቆ
በቀስተ ደመና ሕብራዊ ቀለም ደምቆ
እንደሚተኮስ የሮችት ፍንዳታ
ይንራል ወደ ጠፈር በማታ።
ያ ነው ስሜት፤ ውብ ጎሊና
ጊዜ ሳይሸረው የሚቆይ የሚጸና
በአከናፋቱ ይበራል ወደ ሰማያት
ይንደረድራልም ወደ ታች ቁልቁለት።
ስሜቱ እሳት እንደሚተፋ አቶን
ተስፋን ለመዝራት ሲማስን
ይፈጥራል መንከር ግብር።
ትንግርት ነው ስሜቱ ተአምር።
እንደሚርገበገብ የውቅያኖስ አናት ጫፍ
ጨረር ሲበትን ሲያንጸባርቅ ከአፋፍ
ሲብረቀረቅ እንደ ባዙቃ
ስሜት ሆኖ ወርቃማ ዕቃ።
ኃያል ነው ሕያው ነው ስሜት
ሲነገር፤ ሲተረክ በአንደበት።   (17 Nov 2018)

የዕውቀት ማዕድ ግብዣ

አውቄህ የማላውቅህ
ሳላውቅህ የማውቅህ
ከሩቅ ሆነህ በቅርብ ያለህ
በቅርብ መስለህ ከሩቅ ያለህ

ግና፦
ምን ይሆን ስሜትህ
ምንስ ይሆን ሥጋትህ
እኮ ለምን ይሆን ዝምታህ?

ረሃቡ ሳይጠናብን
ጥማቱ ሳያወረዛን
ፈጥነን እንሂድ ወደ ገነት
ውሃው ወደሚፍለቀለቅበት
የዕውቀት ጥማት ይረካ ዘንድ
ላንቃችን ይረጥብ ዘንድ
እንሰብስብ የዕውቀት አዝመራ
ይከመር በጎተራ
ረሃባችን አንዲያባራ።

ጥማታችን - ረሃባችን ይገታ ዘንድ
እንቂደስ ከዕውቀት ማዕድ። (10 Jan 2019)

ከ «ለገባሯ» ለተፈናቀሉ

ትናንት ዕልልታ፣ ዛሬ እሪታ
ነገ ደስታ፣ ከዚያም ዋይታ
መች ይሆን የሚቆም፣ መች ይሆን የሚያበቃ?
ያገሬ ሰው እንግልትና ሰቆቃ
ከቀዬው ከሰፈሩ ሲሰደድ
የታመሰ ይመስል በእሳት ሰደድ
በወገኑ ሲገፋ ሲፈናቀል
ጭካኔ ነው መቅሰፍት ነው እግዚአ እንበል! (22 Feb 2019)

የተስፉ መደብዘዝ

ነጋ ሲባል መምሽቱ
ቁስሉ ሳይድን ማገርሸቱ
ብርሃን ሲታይ መጨለሙ·
የተስፉ ስሜት መስለምለሙ·
ምን ይሉታል ይህን ሀመም
የማይድን ለዝንተ-ዓለም
ቢያዩት ቢያክሙት ለዘላለም።

የኢትዮጵያ ሥቃይ መከራ
ከቶ የማይፈታ፤ የማያባራ
ቃል ተስፉ መፍትሔ ላይሆን
ምግብ፣ ልብስ፣ ቤት አይሆን።

እንባሽ ይሁን ምስክር
ለቅሶሽ ይሁን የሚናገር
መስከሪ «ለገጣፎ» ባንደበትሽ
ሲደረመስ መኖሪያ ቀዬሽ
በጎሊና-ቢስ ሹሞች ትእዛዝ
ሲፈርዱብሽ እያሉ ያንቺው መዘዝ
የመዘናኛ ቦታ ለማቁም
የመሠረተ ፕላን ትልም
የቱ ይሆን የሚቀድመው
መዝናኛው ይሆን መኖሪያው?   (27 Feb 2019)

የተከሰከሰው EAL ቦይንግ 737 ማክስ 8
(በረራ ቁጥር 302)

አይቀር ነገር ይህ አደጋ
አይተነብዩት ቀን ሲነጋ።

ተቀጠፈ የሰው ሕይወት
በቢሾፍቱ ሰማያት።

ላንዱ ልጅ ለሌላው አባት
ላንዱ ወንድም ወይም እህት
ለሌላው ዘመድ ወይ ጓደኛ
ክቡር ሰው የሁሉም መገናኛ።

ወደ ምድር ድንገት አቅንቶ
ገባ መሬት ሆዷን ከፍቶ
ታላቁ ቦይንግ ግራ ተጋብቶ ።

ውድ ነፍሳት የማይተኩት
መሬት ከፍተው በቢሾፍቱ
አለቁ አሉ ውድ ነፍሳቱ።

ነፍስ ይማር
መንፈስ ይክበር
በደጃፉ፣ በፈጣሪ በር
ይዳሱ የግዜርን ፊት፤ የሱን መንበር። (11 March 2019)

የኢትዮጵያ ዕንቆቅልሽ

ምነዋ ያ የተስፋ ብርሃን ደከመ
ደበዘዘ፣ ተስለመለመ፣ ከሰመ?
ነጋ ሲባል ፈጥኖ ጨለመ?
የፍቅር ስሜቱ ቀዘቀዘ፣ ደከመ፡፡

አዕላፉ ደስታውን ለማብሰር
ትንሣኤውን ባደባባይ ለመናገር
ከዳር እስከዳር በደስታ ፈንድቆ
ወጥቶ ነበር በባንዲራ ደምቆ፡፡

አሁን ደግሞ፡-

ለምን ይሆን ሰቆቃና ግፍ መብዛቱ
አከተመ ሲባል ባዲስ መታየቱ?
ተፈታ ሲባል የሚለው ብቅ
ሞች ይሆን ዕንቆቅልሹ የሚያልቅ?

ዳግም እስኪፈታ እንጠብቅ?
ያ ነው ታላቁ መጠይቅ፡፡ (21 March 2019)

የኮድ ብሉ [Code Blue] ነፍስ አድን ጥሪ

አካል ሲዝል ልብ ሲቆም
ትንፋሽ ሲያጥር ሳንባ ሲደክም
አንጎል ዝሎ ሲስለመለም
ነፍስ ግቢ - ነፍስ ውጪ ሲሆን
የሞት ሽረት ፈተና ሲገን
ዘብ ይቆማል በሕይወት እርከን፡፡
ይጠራል ነፍስ አድን ቡድን፡፡

ያስተጋባል የብርከ ጥሪ
ይደውላል ይጋደፋል እያለ እሪ
ድረሱ ሲል ድምጹ ማጉያው
መላው ቡድን ወደ ጎራው
ወደ ጦርነት ወደ አውድማው
በቅጽበታዊ ላንድ አላማ
ነፍስ ሊታደግ ሕይወት ሊያለማ
ፈጥኖ ይነጉዳል ወደፊት
ወደ ደከመው ታማሚ ሰውነት፡፡

ሞትን ሊያከሽፍ በፍጥነት
ይጋፈጣል ከፊት ለፊት፡፡

ክቡር አካል ከቡሩ ሰው
ተንጋሎ ተዘርግቶ ባልጋው
ደርሶ የነፍስ መለያያው
ቅጥ አምባሩ የጠፋው ልብ
ሲውተፈተፍ ሲርገበገብ
ስርዓት ጠፍቶት ሲተራመስ
ሳንባም ረስቶ በቅጥ መተንፈስ

ውስጠ-አካል ይታገላል ሳይሰለች
ከሞት በላይ ከሕይወት በታች፡፡

በድኑ አካል ሳይናገር ሳይናዘዝ
ይቆማል በሕይወት/ ሞት ጠርዝ
ምንም ሳይል ሳይተነፍስ
ባየር ተንሳፉ ውዲታ ነፍስ
ትላለች ቆሎ ና ቆሎ ድረስ፡፡

ያ ቡድን፡-

ፈጥኖ ደራሽ ይዞ መስመር
ደካማ ልብን ለማጠንከር
ኃይል ለመስጠት ዳግም ለማንዘር
ይገፋል ደረት፣ ይሰጣል መድኃኒት
ደግሞም ይመታል አንዛሪ ሳጥን
ኃይል አፍልቆ ከእምቅ ብርሃን
ልብን በፍጥነት ለማሥራት፡፡

ባፍ ባፍንጫ አየር ይነፋል
እንዳይታፈን ጸንቶ እንዲታገል
ሳንባን ለማገዝ እንዲተነፍስ
እንዲመለስ የሕይወት እስትንፋስ

በላብ ተጠምቆ ሁሉን ሞክሮ
"ነፍስ አድን" ቡድን ዕውቅት አጣምሮ
ጀግና ይወጣል ሞትን ገፍትሮ
ሕይወት ሲመልስ ከሞት አፋፍ ላይ
ከፍያው ያ ነው ውጤቱን ሲያይ
አቤት እርካታ አቤት እፎይታ
ሞትን ድል ነስቶ የማታ ማታ፡፡

በሌላ በኩል፦

ሲያሸንፍ ጣእረ ሞት
በለስ ቀንቶት ሰዓት ቀንቶት
ይ'ፈታል የ «ኮዱ» ጦር
ይመለሳል ወደ ሰፈር
በጥሩ ውጊያው ረክቶ
በትግሉ ጥረት ኮርቶ።

ያ ነው የ «ኮድ ብሉ» መዘክሩ
የጀግኖች፣ ነፍስ አድኖች ስከንሳሩ።   (09 April 2019)

የኛ ዘመን፣ የኛ ጊዜ

በኛ ዘመን፣ በኛ ጊዜ
እየቱባለ ይተረካል በትካዜ
ይህ የማያልቅ «የእኛ» ታሪክ አባዜ
ቅጥ ያጣ፣ ብቻ የጥሩነት ኑዛዜ።
እያሰማ «ወርቃማ» ደወል
የየራሱን ትውልድ ያሞካሻል
ይላል ከሁሉም ይበልጣል፣ ይልቃል።

የበፊቱ ሁሌም የሚሻለው
ወይ ያሁኑ የሚበልጠው
እረ ምን ይሆን መለኪያው?
ማወዳደሪያው ማነፃፀሪያ ሚዛኑ
የዳኝነት መስጫ እርከኑ?
ስብዕና ወይስ የቁስ ብዛት
ሥልጣኔ ወይስ ባህላዊ እሴት
የቱ ነው የሚደፋ ሚዛን?
የሚልቅ ለአንዱ ዘመን።
ጊዜ እንደሁ ወደኋላ አይመለስ
ይነጉዳል ወደ አዲስ አድማስ
ሁሉም ዘመን አለው የራስ ነገር
ከሌላኛው ሲወዳደር ~ ሲነጻጸር።
ጥሩም መጥፎም የሚበየን
የሚወድስ አሊያም የሚኮንን።

ግና፦
መች ይገኛል ሐቀኛ ሚዛን?
የት ይገኛል ያ ፍትሃዊ ዓይን?
አመዛዝኖ የሚሰጥ ብይን። (06 May 2019)

የኢትዮጵያ ሃኪሞች ጥያቄ

ጽልመቱ የሚያልፈው ሌሊቱ የሚነጋው
ጨለማው ተገፎ ብርሃን የሚበራው
ሙት ይሆን ያ ቀን ተስፋ የሚዘራው
የኢትዮጵያ ሃኪሞች ሮሮ የሚሰማው።።   (17 May 2019)

የ ICU መደበኛ ትዕይንት

የህመም ፈተና መናኸሪያ
የሆስፒታል ነፍስ ማቆያ
የጥድፊያ የሕይወት ፍትጊያ
የነፍስ ውጪ የነፍስ ግቢ ፍልሚያ፡፡

መድኃኒት በከረጢት ተሞልቶ
ተንቆርቁሮ አካል ገብቶ
ሰውነትን ሊያስተካክል
በመጠኑም ከፍ ዝቅ ሲል
ይጥራል ጤናማ ለማድረግ
ሳንባ-ልብን ሊታደግ፡፡

በመተንፈሻ መሣሪያ ግፊት
ተለክቶ - ተመጥኖ በትጋት
በቱቦ ይፈሳል ይተኮሳል
በሳንባ አድርጎ ወደ ውስጥ አካል
ኃዋስ ባየር እጦት እንዳይታፈን
እንዳይሰጥም ወደ ዘላለማዊ ሰመመን፡፡

ልክ እንደ «አርኬድ» ጨዋታ
ደወል ሲያቃጭል ሲመታ
የድምፅ የትእዛዝ ጋጋታ
ክፍሉ ይሞላል በሁካታ፡፡
የብዙ መሣሪያ መብራት
ብልጭ ድርግም የሚልበት
ሳያሰልስ የሚውለበለብበት
የልብ - ሳንባ ሥራ የሚታይበት
በቴሌቪዥን - መሰል መስኮት
ቀጭን መስመር የሚርገበገብበት፡፡

76

ሕይወት ለማቆየት
ትግል ጥድፊያ የበዛበት
ያ ክፍል ነው ጉድ ያለበት።
ጣእር ይነግሣል በቾሎ
ትርምስና እርጋታ ተቀላቅሎ
ቤተ - ዘመድ በብርኪ የሚያዝበት
ሁሉም የሚርመሰመስበት
አንዳንዴም መጨረሻው ግልጽ ያልሆነበት
የጤና ጀግኖች የሞሉበት
አያልቅም ቢነገር ባንደበት
ያጣዳፊ-ክፍል (ICU) ትዕይንት። (20 May 2019)

ሃኪሙ ሲታመም

አካሚው ታካሚ ሲሆን
ሃኪም በሌላ ሃኪም ሊድን
ሰጪው ተቀባይ ሲሆን
ዕንቆቅልሹ ምን ይሆን?
ህመም እንደሁ ሰው አይመርጥ
አንዱን ከሌላ ያበልጥ
ሁሉንም በእኩል ያጠቃል
ገፍትሮ ካልጋ ያውላል
ለዚህ ነው ነገ በኔ የሚባል።

እናም ከህመሙ ውጭ ተመልክቶ
የሙያ ግብረ ገብነትን አካቶ
ይጠቅማል መመልከቱ
ህመምተኛን እንደሰውነቱ።
ያኔ ነው ሙያው የሚከበር
ከዕውቀቱ ከምጥቀቱ የሚሻገር።

ከላብራቷር ቁጥር የላቀ
ከውስጥ ምስሉ ርቆ የመጠቀ
ክቡር ነው አካሉ የማይጣስ
የማይገሰስ የማይደፈርስ
በኩራት የታጀበ የደመቀ
ያላለቀ ገና ያልደቀቀ
ሰውነት/ ስብእናው ነው የላቀ የረቀቀ
የህክምናን አድማስ የጣስ የራቀ።   (02 June 2019)

የማይሞት ተስፋ

የቅርብ አካል የሩቅ ምድር
የደም ማገር የዘያ መንደር
ቋሚው ዕትብት የኖረበት
የማይመከን ትልቅ ስሜት
የማይነጥፍ ጥልቅ ፍቅር
ኢትዮጵያ የተአምር ሃገር።

የማይጠፋ የእሳት ነበልባል
የማይረግብ ኃያል ማእበል
ደከመ ሲባል የሚያገሳ
ወደቀ ሲሉት የሚነሳ
እንደ ፊኒክሱ አሞራ
አራግፎ ትቢያ - አቧራ
ሞተ ሲባል ነፍስ ይዘራል
ያንሠራራል ዳግም ይገዝፋል
ጨለም ሲባል ብርሃን ይረጫል።

ግና መች ይሆን የሚቋመው
ችዋ ችዌው የሚቀረው?
የሚሰክነው የሚጠፋው። (08 July 2019)

ደመና ሲጋልብ

ነጭ ደመና ሲጋልብ
በነጎድጓድ ድምጽ አጀብ
ተንሳፈፌ በበራሪ ምንጣፍ
በምናብ እንደ ጆፌ ስከንፍ
ደምቃ ተከባ በሰማይ ጀንጥላ
ምድሪቱ ከበታች ተንጣላ
ያን ደጋን ቀስተ ደመና
ሳየው በተመስጦ በጥሞና
ሉብሶ አረንጓዴ ቢጫ ቀይ
መሬት ነክቶ ታኮ ሰማይ

ምንኛ ያረካል
ሕይወትን ያድሳል
ኢትዮጵያ ያስብላል
ያ ከፉ ቀን ያልፋል። (22 July 2019)

የብራዚል/ የአማዞኑ እሳት

ምነዋ ብራዚል ነደድሽ ተቃጠልሽ?
በእሳት ተንቀለቀልሽ ተጠበስሽ?
ምንኛ ያስከፋል ያሳዝናል
ማየቱ ያን ጥፋት ያን ነበልባል
እንዲያ ሲግም ሲጠፋ ደኑ
የተፈጥሮ ሃብት መምከኑ
በውስጡ ያሉት እንስሳት
የመድኃኒት ምንጭ ዕጽዋት
ሲጠፋ ተንጨርጭረው ዓመድ ሲሆኑ
ሆድ ይሰብራል ነባላሉ እርግማኑ
ከብራዚል ዘልቆ የዓለም ሃብት
ወሳኝ ጠባቂ የአየር ንብረት
መካነ ሕይወት-ብዝሃ ሕይወት
ያሳዝናል *መመልከት ያን ውድመት።* (24 Aug 2019)

የግጥም ሃይል

ነበልባል ነው፣ ነዲድ ነው ስሜቱ
ፍም ነው፣ እሳት ነው አንደበቱ
ቃላት አምጦ፣ ከእምቁ አፍልቆ
ተፈጥሮን ዘከረ በምናቡ አድንቆ።   (03 Sept 2019)

ለሺካጎ የድኅረ ምረቃ ትምህርት አስተማሪዬ (NRF)

የተባ ነበር ብዕሩ፣ ርቱዕ ነበር አንደበቱ
የገነነ፣ የመጠቀ ነበር ዕውቀቱ
ተካትቶ በእትመት ከምችቱ
በስብሰባ መድረክ አቅርቦቱ
እሱ ነው የማለዳው፣ የጥዋቱ።

በክፍል፣ በላብራቷር ምርምር
ሩጫ ባለበት፣ በበዛበት ግርግር
አካል ሲዝል፣ አእምሮ ሲደክም
በቅርብ ሆኖ አይዞህ በርታ ሲል
ተስፋ አይነጥፍም ጥረት ሲግል።

ቀን አያርፍም ማታ አይተኛም
ከሳይንስ ጥያቄ ሲፋለም ሲላተም
መፍትሔ ሊሻ ሲማስን ሲደክም
ያልተነገረለት ያልተዘመረለት
ጀግና ነው የማይፈርስ ሐውልት
እሱ ነበር የማይሰለች የማይታክት።

በተማሪው ቀርጾ ቋሚ ትዝታ
ትውልድ ተሻግሮ በሐሳብ ትውስታ
ይኖራል ይዘልቃል ጊዜ ሳይፈታው
ዘመን ሳይረሳው፣ ጊዜ ሳይሽረው። (08 Sept 2019)

የብዕርና የሕይወት ጉዞ

አልወየበም ላህዩ፣ አልነጠፈም ብዕሩ
አልሰለለም ልሳኑ፣ ጥብቅ ነው ያንጎል ከሩ
ትንግርት ነው ያ ቄመናው ያ ምግባሩ።

የሕይወትን ወጀብ ነጎድጓድ
የአመዳይን ንጥፈ በረድ
ተቋቁሟል ሳይወድ በግድ።

አይችለው የለ የሰው ፍጡር፣
ምን ይሳነው በዚህ ምድር
ተሸክሞ ሥቃይ፣ ችግር?

ህልም አልሞ ተስፋን አዝሎ
ባዲስ መንፈስ ቀኑን ውሎ
ይማስናል ሁሉን ችሎ።

ሲጨልም የሕይወት ፀዳል
ከንግዲህስ ምን ቀረኝ ሲል
በቃኝ ይላል መንፈስ አካል።   (14 Sept 2019)

መወድስ ለሳይንቲስቶች

በረጅም ትምህርት ተጉዛችሁ
የዕውቀት ኦድማስን አስፍታችሁ
በቤተ ሙከራ ውላችሁ፣ አድራችሁ

ችግርን ለመታደግ ለመወጣት
በማስረጃ፣ በጠንካራ ጥናት
ቆማችሁ በማይናወጥ መሠረት
ቀን ከሌት ስትደከሙ ስትዋትሩ
ዓለምን ልታወጡ ከድክመቱ
ከአባዜው፣ ከዕውቀት ድህነቱ

ማን ያውቃል ማን ይ'ረዳል?
የናንተን ድካም የናንተን ጌድል
ተወስኖ በራሱ ሰፈር፣ በራሱ ክልል።
ብቻ አሻራችሁ የሚታይ
ልፋታችሁ ከሁሉም በላይ
የሚያበራ እንደ ብሩህ ፀሐይ።

መዐልት - ምሽት ሳይሆን እንቅፋት
ስታበስሩ፣ ስታውጁ አዲስ ግኝት
ያ ነው የናንተ ቋሚ ሽልማት።

ሲሰበር የዕውቀት ዳር ድንበሩ
በምናባዊ ደመና በደስታ ስትበሩ
ያ ነው የናንተ መከፈልቱ፣ መዘከሩ።
ሳይንቲስቶች ከበሩ፣ ኩሩ!   (16 Oct 2019)

የኮሮና ወረርሽኝን ለሚታገሉ

ይህ ኮቪድ የሚሉት ጉድ
መላውን ዓለም ሲያንዳግድ
መነሻው መድረሻው የማይታወቅ
ሕይወት ሲቀጥፍ ሃገር ሲያደቅ
ይህ መቅሰፍት ደቂቅ ሕዋስ
ግዙፉን ሰው ሲፈታተን ሲያምስ።

ይወለዳል ይፈልቃል ኀበዝ ጀግና
ሊታገል ሊዋጋ ደቂቁን ኮሮና
በመንገድ ባደባባይ በሆስፒታል
ጦርነቱ ሳያሰልስ ይቀጥላል።   (19 March 2020)

Part 2

Poems in English

Day and Night

Sunrise and sunset;
Day and night;
Time swings back and forth like the pendulum;
To signify the interminable continuum.

(22 April 2019)

On the Paradox of Love
(Philosophical Free Verse)

Love is like a mirage;
Close up, it disappears.

Love is like the moon;
Look up, it waxes and wanes.

Love is like the ocean tide;
Observe, it peaks and dips;
It rises and falls.

Love is like the weather;
It is at once hot and cold;
Like a volcano, or an ice crater.

Love is an indeterminate sentiment;
It climaxes and bottoms;
A crescendo and decrescendo.

Love is all how one feels;
About physical and inner beauty;
It evades logic and reason without reason.

Love is inexplicable;
Maybe, a mere alignment of comfort.

Unequal love is contorted;
Twisted and deformed;
Amounts to an empty shell;
Prone to crack and implode.

(03 Dec 2018)

New Year

As we get ready to say goodbye to an Old Year and
welcome a New Year to the present;
Memory stretches back to the good and the bad to reflect.

Perfection was never meant to be within man's province;
Nevertheless, in a 20-20 hindsight we conjure up a
scenario akin to that stance.

For what it is, Old Year belongs to the past;
New Year begins to shape the present.

Grasp the New Year with hope and determination;
To live the coming days and months with exaltation.

Put on a genuine and luminous face;
Top it with an arresting gesture of peace.

Surmount difficulties with optimism and hard work;
Knowing that bad days will be of the past to be anchored
for good to the dock.

Raise up high your mast, sail with the wind;
To a self-promised land, past the horizon beyond.

Consider the year as a day's journey;
Rise up with the Sun to plunge into the day.

Plough through bad weather day and move on with grace with the winds;
Follow your day as the Sun travels to the horizon to set beyond the earth radiating golden rays;

Yes, rays spiked and projected in a firework style into the skies.

Let the New Year roll in, amid snow, cold and inclement, or even nice weather;
No matter what, welcome it with candor!

(Dec 2017)

A Tribute to Facebook

Oh Facebook,
How close thou have brought folks together,

How intimate and yet remote thy pronouncements have been to ears and eyes near and yonder.

I have witnessed thee, that is, how at the same time exaggerative and superficial thou can be,

How powerfully thou connect relatives, Acquaintances and long forgotten and lost friends that only the mental eyes could see.

Thou have graced thy pages with images of beauty, sorrow, happiness, laughter, tears, knowledge, the moons, the stars, politics, economics---all manners of potpourri issues,

Only thou, Facebook, know how to criss-cross various interests with respectable boundaries.

Overall, I rate thee excellent, for ye have brought the best out of the multitudes!!!   (Jan, 2016)

Sunrise and Sunset

In all its glory, the Sun rises;
Casting its golden rays;
Heralding a new day, a fresh dream;
Replete with undying optimism;
Own the day; don't be led astray;
When the long day ends;
As it ceremoniously closes;
Chase the flirtatious Sunset;
As the Sun rushes to the West;
To sink into the horizon beyond;
Declaring the day's cyclical end;
Into the dark skies of the night;
With a beautiful twilight;
To the seductive ball of fire;
Say "good-night" to the rosy aura of Nature.

(10 July 2019)

On a Day the Sun Rains

On a sweltering day in summer;
When butterflies greet you with color;
The Sun rains down its rays;
Piercing through beautiful azure skies;
Yet, the breeze knocks off the warm stings;
A walk on the trails of Perry Creek;
It is refreshing and therapeutic.
With deers wandering in the grass;
As if to greet you from a distance;
What a day to pass!
In the company of beautiful Nature;
One wishes it lasted forever.

(13 Aug 2019)—Sioux City, IA

Heroes and Heroines of COVID-19

In the science of optometry;
The designation 20/20;
Represents optical purity;

In the field of health history;
The year 2020;
Signifies a year of infamy;
An ugly sight and so blurry;
Filled with death and agony.

A year so dreaded;
Despised and detested;
A year of COVID;
All over the world.

A year of despair and panic;
Violating a human characteristic;
Distancing reigning over proximity;
So as to deny the contagion easy entry;
Into the sacred human body.

Yet, the spirit of mankind;
Shined in the dark nights all around;
In Lombardy and all over Italy;
Folks sang from balconies in solidarity.

All across Europe standing on balconies;
Lighting candles in dark COVID nights;
Citizens hailed heroes and heroines;
Health personnel of all cues;
Who battled the corona virus.

Health workers across nations;
Working hard to curb the virus;
Made touching public appeal;
To stay home away from peril;
While they fought the tiny evil;
In hospital wards behind curtains;
Risking their own lives.

Let's be proud of all mankind;
Of all good people across the world.

(24 March 2020)

Part 3
Memory Notes

Newsmen of Yester year

It was an envied, if not the most envied, profession. It was a trade reserved only for the gifted (probably not as much for the well-trained). All newsmen were lumped under the generic vernacular name "*gazetegnotch.*" It would also include news-reporters. Television was not that common. Printed materials were the way to go--a rule rather than the exception. Among contributors to *Dimts* (Voice) and *Addis Zemen* (New Era) gazettes, Paulos Gnogno stands out tall (bless his soul!). I think he was an autodidact--a self-taught intellectual. His short and precise answers to questions from readers (*a'nd tiyake alegn amd*=I Have a Question) were indeed memorable. The *Ethiopian Herald* used to be the premier and the only English daily news organ in the country. Of course, there was one Yacob Woldemariam, whose incisive articles were unforgettable. The *Herald* was his baby, after having taken over editorship from the African-American editor David Talbot. There were also magazines such as the *Amargna* "*Menen*" and the famous English "*Addis Reporter*," which (the latter) was always the talk of the town, especially among the elite. Oh boy, *Arat Kilo* has seen its own share of the literary cream of the day in its heyday! Contributors to *Addis Reporter* were people of the caliber of Solomon Deressa, Gedamu Abraha, Sebhat Gebre-Egziabeher and others. The magazine span articles on literature, education, and various critiques.

Unfortunately, it died untimely death after 3 or 4 years of publication.

In the English news broadcast time slot, I remember Yilma Feleke, Leulseged Kumsa, Haimanot Alemu, Aweitu Simeso, Romaneworq Kassahun, etc. Among notable *Amarigna* newscasters were the famed Asaminew Gebrewold, Solomon Bekele and later others like Teklu Tabor, and much later Tadesse Muluneh.

Way back in my green years, I used to be glued to our first Philips transistor radio my late father ever owned, especially early on when following news of the abortive *coup de tat* of B/General Mengistu Neway. At "*sebategna*" mini-square in *Addis Ketema* (Addis Ababa), right at a crossroad, there was a tall pole on which a loudspeaker was mounted. People from the area used to gather there to listen to the blaring radio, while getting their shoes polished---especially on Sundays.

One rainy night in *Addis* Ababa

The rainy season in *Addis* used to be no fun. The late famed singer *Tilahun Gesesse* called it "*ye Hamle Chilema*=the dark month of July)" in one of his classic romantic songs. We hated to be wet (being soaked head to toe) in the heavy downpours of the monsoon season. Of course, if you happen to wear shoes with holes in them, you would be in big trouble. Don't even think of being decked out in your best outfit; would be almost a "suicidal" feat, so to write. Taxis scurrying around town at a maddening speed would get close to the side of the road and splash the muddy water all over you----some on purpose. Good grief! It would ruin the whole day, especially for the fair sex. Mind you, there was no sufficient drainage to capture the run-off, nor sidewalks to keep oneself at a safe distance.

    I don't like thunders, even to this day. They scare the heck out of me. When I was a kid, I used to take a night winter class (off-season) in the early 1960's at a school which was only a stone-throwing distance from our house in *Addis Ketema, Addis Ababa*. The night class used to be dismissed around 8 pm. One such night, there was a torrential rain with a blinding thunder lighting up the night sky of *Addis* with a ferocious and fearsome noise. I started running home as fast as my legs could carry me to avoid being drenched. I thought I was in a wet roasting inferno---made it safe to my house, but frightened to death, despite having not being struck by a seemingly "deadly" lightning. My late mom took me to her cuddling and warm embrace, assuring me everything was all right, son!

Whenever I think of the monsoon rainy season (*Kiremt*) in *Addis,* those memories flash back in my head, although I am a good dozens of years removed from it--I mean that particular rainy night in *Addis.* Oh *Addis*, how much I loved you! I saw in your womb all manner of people from all over the country; you were indeed a true melting pot, figuratively and literally, that is!

The Afro hair-styled "gate-man" (*Gofer*)

This memory takes me back to my so-green days at *Wossen Seged* Elementary School in Addis Ababa. One of the memories that stands out in my formative years then was our so-called main-gate guard who went by the nickname *Gofer*. His real name, if distance memory doesn't fail me, was Tessema. *Gofer*, because he wore his hair fearsome long and it was salted and peppered, so to write. His short yet muscular physique armed with his "deadly" whip (*gumare*) used to strike terror among the kids at *Wossen Seged* elementary school. When teachers wanted to hand down a severe punishment, they would send students to his "mercy." Also, I remember a long and cemented basin-like sink which would capture (drain out) water from a faucet. Drinking water from that faucet was considered a privilege. Don't ask me why. We used to place a lookout for *Gofer* while thirsty lads took a hurried gulp of water to quench their thirst. If some-how he snuck upon you, you would get a flurry of lashes, which you have to frantically and literally outrun. I never understood why he did that. Don't ever think of showing up late at the school gate, lest you faced the much-dreaded lashes of *gumare*. Well, those were the days, ladies and gents. On the flip and happier side of it, a few hundred feet in the back of the school, there was an adorable old lady we used to call *Emama Adeshe*, *adesh"e* being a wheat bread (*mulmul dabo*) that she would sell you for astronomical five cents. Usually, you would sit in her tukul and she would present it to you sprinkled with red pepper. A couple or more students would share a piece and get satisfied. We would then go to our respective homes merrier and singing, as if *Gofer* never existed in the Cosmos. *Emama Adeshe* was so kind and talked to the school kids with affection, respect and care, although you may call it "business." My foot, a 5-cent business! The memory lives on.

Parents' Day

When I was growing up, some of the happiest times of my elementary/junior high days were during the festivities of so-called Parents' Day at the end of School Year. The biggest projects in preparation for Parents' Day, I recall, used to be carving (sculpting) all kinds of imaginary birds out of cow's/oxen horns, and weaving a cover around wine bottles (used to be called *fashkets*).

The horns from dead cows/oxen for bird-carving were obtained by scouring the nooks and corners of *Addis Ketema*. You would find them scattered/strewn around in most parts of Addis, and all you had to do was find the ideal one with the right size and curvature. Of course, you would have to have the right kind of tools, such as tiny saws, sandpaper and the final polishing material when you go to the nitty gritty stage of the actual sculpting. If your work was lucky enough to be selected by the handicraft teacher, it would be displayed for sale on Parents' Day---big deal! You would feel so achieved and proud. I was a so-so kid in that department and my work never made it to the "sell" status. The other most common handicrafts work was to make a cover around bellied wine bottles (a la *ye tej birile*), by knitting carefully colored, bundled, braided, and woven sisal around the bottle -- required patience and skill. It was a favorite project of my classmate and friend in Grade 5.

End-of-school year parties managed by the school administration were theatrical and quite interesting--there were self-proclaimed Tilahun Gassesse wannabes, who roamed from one classroom to the other entertaining other kids-----some really were good. The Sudanese singers Mohamed Werdi and Saeed Khalifa were also of repute in those days. Some kids even sang the popular hits of these stars ("*Seberta*" comes to mind). Mind you, there was no talent show in those days, as they are proliferative nowadays.

Well bygone days are gone in the merciless time-warp. Yet, I prefer clinging to the happy memories!

The *Pari Mode* Era

Long skirts were common for the fair sex of the era. That was in keeping with the tradition of the *ancien'* days. Pants and jeans were unheard of. Forget about bikinis, tops and blouses that show parts of the upper body. Bikinis? You must be kidding; relatively speaking, beachless and pool-less Addis Ababa was not meant for that kind of fashion after all. In the skirt department, however, dresses were surreptitiously and seductively climbing upstairs to the knee-line turning to miniskirts—yet, they were frowned upon, especially by the older conservative class of the society. Then, there was the ***"PariMode"*** Paris Mode era—a fashion akin to the broader mini-skirt category.

I was once reminded by a friend of an official couplet in a song which ran:

Pari mode lebsaletch shurab deribaletch;
Tseguruan tetekusa, se'at adrgaletch

It roughly translates into:
Clad in Paris-mode dress and sweater;
She wore a watch with styled hair.

In a local *Merkato* version of the same lyrics of the Ethiopian oldie, I remember the couplet ran something like:

PariMode Lebsalech, Silicha
Shurab derbaletch, kotitcha

Translation:
Garbed in a sac-like Paris-Mode dress;
With her top, she was a cotton mess.

    This was, of course, by way of de-condoning the rising fashion of the era. Later, it turned vogue. Fashion has, for sure, evolved over the years! I am told it goes in a circle, backpedaling to resurrect old styles.

Epiphany (*Timqet*)

Here is a short recollection of *Timqet* from my memory bank, and along with it, a funny incident which may, or may not make you smile. You are all familiar with the festive mood around *Timqet*--a religious festival where thousands upon thousands of Orthodox church followers would take to the streets and footpaths escorting their respective Arks to a place called *Timqete bahir*. I believe it was in January, on *St* Michael's day. BTW, as a side bar, my Christian name, I was told by my late mother, was Seife Michael after the St. that she used to love, and to whom she would promise all sorts of gifts (*silets*) (on our behalf, her children) in the form of alms to beggars, and incense (*itan*), myrrh (*kerbe*) and beeswax candle (*t'uaf*) to the church.

Boys, girls, and grown-ups as well, would sing jubilantly as they trail behind the procession. For me, the highlight of *Timqet* was always to watch the clergy sing, with the beats of drums piercing the otherwise still air, with the sistrum (*tsenatsl*) clinking in a hypnotizing fashion, and all well-choreographed and blended with a breathtaking dance of the priests, cross-staffs (*mequamia*) held at a near-perfectly lined-up angle in their hands. An awesome sight to behold!

Back to the funny anecdote; by the time the procession reached our area on its way to a creek, past St Emmanuel church, the priest (among many) carrying an

Ark on his head suddenly stopped. Nobody knew what was going on. The crowd thought that the Ark was not happy about something, and they started to pray. No sooner the crowd noticed a tiny dog which snuck into the crowd was pulling on the trousers and paraphernalia (*albasat*) of the priest carrying the ark. The revelation came when the dog to the surprise of everybody barked its way out. Thusly, the mystery self-debunked itself in a dramatic manner, and in clear view. Not to take away anything from anybody, yet it was indeed funny---and we laughed about the incident for years thereafter, whenever we remembered it.

Ethiopian New Year (*Enqutatash*)

Well,"*felagi abeba, felagi abeba*" was a loud selling-call that would echo in the neighborhoods on *enqutatash,* as kids (not excluding me, of course) roamed around blocks and corners of *Addis Ketema* (Addis Ababa) trying to sell their colorful, picture-laden posters (hand-drawn); the memory trip this time around is to the close of the 1950's (or the beginning years of the 1960's) [Greg Cal]. *Addis amet* (aka *q'dus yohan's; r'ese awde amet; enqutatsh*) is one of the most joyous and memorable holidays in Ethiopia for me (then), as it is, 'm sure, for most people. You would sell each drawing for five, ten or fifteen cents (*amist, asir* or *haya amist santim*), depending on the size and the quality of the poster. To the buyers (other kids who did not have the talent or resources to prepare their own drawings), the posters would bring them about twice the amount that they had paid for them, when they received money from relatives and neighbors after presenting these precious *enqutatash* gifts.

    I vividly recall the intense preparation that went into colored posters, "*abeba,*" starting with the purchase of ink powder, the various sized plain-white paper cuts, and so-called designs. The designs were basically outlines (such as depiction of St. Gabriel, a lion, lady Ethiopia, *Janhoy,* etc.). They were made by special talented hands---artists. One would make a tracing by laying the design on top of so-called carbon paper, which in turn would rest on the plain paper. With the outline traced, we would prepare the ink (various colors) by dissolving the powder in a certain volume of water to a required consistency and brightness. We used to make our own Q-tips, which would be our improvised brush to dip into the prepared ink and rub into the body of the designs with various colors while carefully staying within the borders. Tell you, was meticulous and fun---at least a 3-day work, though---by the time you dried the final products!

Actually, the "seed money" for the preparation of "*abeba*" would be saved early on from *buhe* (*Debre Tabor, Nehasse 13)* holiday that came towards the conclusion of the monsoon rainy season (mid-*Nehasse*). *Buhe* was of course another joyful celebration, especially for us then kids. Truth be told, I didn't know at that time the reason for the holiday (the day Jesus revealed himself to his disciples, I learned later), except for the fact that we always looked forward to it, in anticipation of forming chant groups (each, 5- or 6-membered) in preparation for *buhe*. Then, starting at about mid-day, armed with sticks (*dula*) we would chant (sing) by going from house to house in the neighborhood, and far out if we were brave enough. The *dula* would serve the dual purpose of providing background music to our chants by thumping it on the wooden floors of homes, and also for chasing away unfriendly dogs who may get in the way. The chanting would run like "*Hoya, hoye---Sabisa, ye wenzew sabisa lisetegn tenesa bale meto hamsa; chim chim yadis Kete lijoch leteb aymechum.....Kber besnde kber betef meqegnah yirgefe inde qola wef; indihu indalachu ayeleyachu indihu indalen ayleyen,* etc. On the other hand, you would hurl out some curse words if you were not rewarded with a cylinder-shaped piece of bread (*dabo*) or "loose" change. We would devour the *'mulmul dabbo's"* through the night when group members congregated for sleep-over in our small house. We would count the money collected and divide it up among ourselves. Each kid could make as much as 3 or 4 *bir*; that is the money that would go into buying the raw materials that I mentioned for *enqutatash* preparation.

Not sure how much of that tradition has since changed or endured over the years. For me, that memory of the kid-celebratory mood of *enqutatash* lives on fresh and for-ever.

Tarzan

The period was during the beginning years of 1970's at Haile Selassie I University (HSIU), *Arat Kilo* campus. Don't ask me the reason why he was called *Napoleon*, for I know not, nor did I ever care to know his real name. For sure, physique-wise he was not as short as Mr. Bonaparte, that French midget of a man. Be that as it may, he was a breakfast/lunch/supper-line inspector at *Arat Kilo* campus cafeteria, under the beloved *Meto Aleqa*. You cut the line, *Napoleon* would sneak upon you, and yank you out to the tail end of the line. *Napoleon's* tolerance to such behavior was understandably directly proportional to your level of seniority on campus. If freshman-*ly* (and sophomoric) you were, he would treat you with less "respect." It was customary in those days to cut a lunch line for reasons of time, or simply as a matter of being rude and disorderly.

In any event, our friend *Tarzan* (his real name—initials YA)—a nickname because I think he liked Tarzan movies—was not a habitual line-cutter. But when he did, let no one dare tell him not to. He was very dark-skinned with big blood-shot eyes. He could stare down the devil herself. One afternoon lunch time, *Napoleon* followed *Tarzan* to the spot in the middle of a long line where we were at. *Tarzan* rolled his big eyes in its socket, muttered something inaudible, and in I-am-serious manner scared away poor *Napoleon*. Since then, *Napoleon* would avoid *Tarzan* at any cost.

By the way, years later YA acquired his medical degree, and today he is an outstanding clinician in Ethiopia, and a top medical researcher in AIDS.

Yeneta Zeleqe

He was quite a character, yet a very learned teacher *"memhir"* in the ecclesiastical sense. He was old for the time (maybe in his late 40's). His name was Zeleke Bewnetu. I remember that he had penned several *"sem/qine"* (wax and gold) lines in an old collection (poetry book). The title of the book escapes me. He used to be *yeAmarigna* (Ethiopian vernacular) teacher in Grade 8. He was unequalled in Ge'ez and wax/gold (*Qine*). Students used to be amused by his personality, though. He always sported his snow-white and embroidered shawl (*netela*), with his signature trousers, *tenefanef Teferi suri*. A few mischievous girls used to sit in the back of the classroom. Yeneta Zeleke liked walking through the aisles between the columns of desks to check pupils' work. So, these girls would pull on his *netela* as he made his way to the back of the room. He would *know* who did it. He would suddenly turn around and say, "*Bal'en godahu bila 'entnwan' beinchet wegatch.*" In fact, the whole class would break into a roaring laughter. Yeneta would be satisfied knowing that he retaliated by making a mockery of them, and that the class responded the way it did.

At another time, he was teaching grammar (*sewa'swu*). It was about drawing a distinction between conjunction (*meste'tsamir*) and preposition (*mestewadid*). He always liked to dramatize while teaching the subject. One example he used to describe preposition was to carry a chair on his head, calling himself a "noun" and the chair a "preposition." On another occasion, while he was teaching sem'ina worq (wax and gold), he kneeled down and ducked under a huge table in the front part of the classroom while he almost put himself out of view. He asked the class if anybody could see him. By hiding, he meant to have turned himself to "*worq*" (gold) in the literary sense. One bright student (yes, he was bright!) shouted that he could see the tip of his *netela*. Yeneta was so infuriated by the retort that he ejected the poor kid from the class, by uttering, "C'mon out you mischievous = *na wuta ante tenkolegna.*" Oh yes, so many interesting stories about Yeneta Zeleke----------,

Before senility descends upon me full force, let me spare a few more seconds to narrate more about *Yeneta* Zeleke. He continued teaching *Amarigna* in Grade 9. He had one funny and strange encounter with one Getachew. Student Getachew hated the academic part of school life, but he loved the social part it. So, didn't give a hoot what he was being taught or what was expected of him. *Amarigna* was not his forte, either. Come end of the last term, *Yeneta* flunked Getachew by giving him less than 40 out of 100. *Amarigna was* one of the compulsory subjects he had to pass. On top of that, he had had problems with other subjects, as well. Well, Getachew's option was to implore *Yeneta* to please cushion him up a little bit, so he would pass *Amarigna*, and smooth-sail to the next grade. He thought if he had a pass in the subject, he could barely pull it off on his total average to pass to the next grade. *Yeneta,* however, wouldn't flinch. At the end of one of the school days, he would follow *Yeneta* outside of the school on his way home, literally begging him to pass him. *Yeneta* stood his grounds. Getachew had had enough! So, in desperation he yelled "F you!" in *Amargna*. You could imagine how a traditional, conservative and celebrated *Yeneta* Zeleke would react to that tornadic outburst. He was caught off-guard and dumb-founded, if not devastated. He repeated after himself the tirade "*Ine, Ine, Lib......*??" and strode off as fast as his legs could carry him. *Yeneta* was overwhelmed; Getachew didn't get a pass and ended up repeating the year! How tragic, both lost!

Of an Old Wedding

It may sound awfully old or recent when I write about "old weddings." It all depends on the eyes/age of the beholder, and how far back one may want to go; but it is still old enough in my eyes. By now, EEDN would have some idea where I hail from---of course, from Ethiopia--- here for the sake of my memory, I would specifically say from *Addis Ketema* on the outskirts of the ever-unforgettable *Merkato*. A caveat: no village "*sefer*" or region mentality, on my part.

Well, that out of my way, what I will try to recount in this entry is my reminiscence about my two older sisters' wedding ceremony as I remember it (wedded the same day) in the early 1960's (Greg Cal). I think a few years later, the more affluent members of the society began throwing wedding parties (in tandem with home festivities, or as separate events) in hotels, such as Hotel d'Afrique, *Wabi Shebelle*, etc, of course always adorned with music from erstwhile big-name singing bands. Our family was not dirt-poor, and yet somewhat close to the bottom of middle societal stratum. Hence, my parents, just like their contemporaries in the area, had saved up enough (call them frugal or what) for such big events as wedding, etc.

The year was 1964, about 2 years after the death of *Itege* Menen. I remember the wedding was postponed from an earlier date, because some government directive was issued, if my memory serves me right, to the effect that weddings were supposed to be put on hold/postponed until the national mourning period for the deceased Empress was complete. In any event, preparation for the wedding went into full swing. *Id'r* (a community-based cooperation group) was a powerful instrument through which families (as members) in the area would be allowed to use utensils (such as metal cups [*kubaya*] and China's) and old-fashioned tents for such ceremonies. The house we owned was small, but the compound on which the property sat, was expansive enough by the standard of the period. I remember there was a wide and open space to the west of our house where tents were pitched for the ceremony. Erecting a tent was an arduous task as some of you may remember. The poles would have to be held in place at certain apexes with the tent opened up, and wooden pegs would be placed at strategic corners on the ground. To the firm pegs would be tied strings coming out of different locations of the hem circling the tent. The synchronized erection of the tent required the strong arms of adults. As kids, we (I, my brother and others) would have fun watching the grown-ups putting it together and lifting the "mammoth" baby! For the wedding (a week or so prior), three contiguous tents were put up to accommodate a relatively large number of invited guests. The more fun part for us was sleeping in the tent on eucalyptus tree leaves and sprinkled *qetema* on the grass-covered ground. Grown-ups would also be assigned to sleep there to ward off human and animal intruders. Guess what the animal intruders were? Hyenas. Yes, hyenas. In those days, just a little further down from our house was a densely wooded area, where the nocturnal guys (hyenas) roamed and resided. They owned the night as it was their food hunting time, when they would venture out into human habitats to look for all sorts of carcass. As one would expect, around wedding times there will be some post-slaughter parts (pathologists may call it post-mortem parts after harvest!) thrown around carelessly, which would attract hyenas. At one time, there was even a newspaper article where the hyenas were hailed in Addis for doing the diligent work that they accomplished on behalf of Municipal Administration in cleaning up (ate) the remains all kinds animals scattered in the city. Coming back to the topic, one night we heard from the tent a close howling of a hyena (s). At a distance, we noticed the twinkling eyes of the hyena in the dark. A close-up shining of a flashlight chased away the unhappy scavenger.

 I remember the regimentation of work for the wedding; some assigned to traditional beer, honey-wine, stew, utensil, flat-bread sections --*tella bet, tej bet, wot bet, iqa atabi bet, injera bet,* and you name the *"bet."* Each assigned person made sure the resource was not depleted and that it ended up at the right destination in the different quarters of the tent. For example, not everybody would be served *tej*, or if served, no repeat (second-round) would be allowed. The air used to be filled with aroma. It felt like wedding to the all the senses. What a nice a memory to carry with me for life!

Of *Gesho Terra*

It was eons ago during the ice age ---- primordial/dinosaurian times, if you are inclined to use these phrases, like I do. A little exaggeration here! Allow me, and cut me slack, please? I was barely more than a "toddler" then, if you will :)-.

Gesho terra in the heart of *merkato* in the vicinity of 7th Police Station, and *wube bereha*, a little out from the back alleys of *Genete Leul* Imperial residence (later HSI University) come to mind. At the time, both were known as hot spots (red light areas) for the young and young-hearted Addis Ababans who liked to dance the night away. Call it whatever you like--the *Rise and Fall of Decadent Culture*, or something to that effect---fact is, it was there, and the youth flocked to it when darkness fell. I may be wrong; I think the *piazza* and *nefas silk* red districts were later arrivals; what do I know?

I remember vividly the *gesho terra* area, as if it was to-day. Music would blare out from the inside of dance clubs (houses). The doors were in the form of strung narrow metal plates, which one would part with a clinking noise by the stretch of the arms, while entering. The door fee would run in the vicinity of 50 *santim*, or less. The dance would go on even on Sunday mornings in the *gesho terra* quarters. *Wube bereha* was usually for the "elite," yet accessible to anyone who can afford one *bir,* or so. Speaking of *gesho terra*, allow me to detour you to *berbere terra* on the way to *Tekelehaymanot* area. You would sneeze your way out, as you walked through the *berebere*-dust saturated noxious air. Obviously, there was a *berbere*-crushing and pounding mill (*weftcho bet*) on one side of the street. A little before you reach there, you would transverse the so-called *merrisa terra*. Oh, these "*terras*"--there were plenty of them! Anyway, there you see brave souls lined up in *kosso* catering houses waiting for their turn to gulp down a canful of tapeworm remedy (*kosso medhanit*) in a well-choreographed ritual, to cleanse their guts of the much-despised and tabooed tapeworm infestation.

Little did I know then, ladies and gents, that some 48 years and two children later, and a turbulent Atlantic-ocean away I would write about this all-Ethiopian taenicide and much more. Oh, well *Mom* Destiny can sail you anywhere She wants, way so far out, beyond the horizon that even the mental eyes cannot ever fathom. It is a pre-ordained destiny from above, I guess, or is it not?!

In closing, back to *wube bereha*. It was an adventure (perhaps wrongly so, in today's eyes) to spend a night in *wube bereha*---one would talk about it for a week, as if it were a monumental accomplishment. Well, that was then. Today is a different animal.

Qirtcha and *Figna*

I don't know to what extent today oxen are slaughtered in Addis neighborhoods (*sefer*) and elsewhere, and the resultant meat apportioned to participants of the meet-parceling (*qircha*) project. Back then, used to happen a lot on holidays, such as End of Lent Season, *Addis Amet, Mesqel,* etc. Growing up, I used to revel in the whole exercise of *qircha*. I think the main idea was that it would be cheaper to participate in *qircha* than buying meat at the butchers. Be that as it may, early in the process the coordinators of the *qircha* would gather a consensus as to how many households in the neighborhood would participate, and then buy the ox. Probably, after the *qircha* was said and done, the coordinators would extract some profit--- kind of a business, too.

    On the slaughter day, the trick was to tie up the poor animal and tackle him (her) to the ground without taxing casualty on the executioners (the Ethiopian equivalents of Spanish matadors). A single mis-step, one could easily be gored. One is reminded of Spanish bullfighting, the difference being in the former it was not sport but a communal ox-kill for the coveted meat. As kids, of course, we were not allowed to get close to the wide circle where the action took place. Once the poor animal is on the ground, the rest of the exercise would follow. Out of respect to the animal rights-minded, I would spare you the gory details you all are familiar with anyway. By the way, I was introduced to rudimentary anatomy observing the process in the "field".

Looking back, it was amazing how little it took to thrill us kids then. Our prize after the ritual was consummated was to be awarded the "*figna*." The *figna* was the urinary bladder of the poor animal, which we would thoroughly wash out clean. I guess it was supposed to be a "balloon" of sorts. We would be lucky if the "*figna*" was not punctured. We would blow air into it and use it as a soccer ball, volleyball, and what not. That was the climax of the process for us, other than helping our parents carry our respective portions of the *qirtcha* home.

Oh, how sweet and memorable those days were!

Senbete

I am sure the "*senbete*" feast was ubiquitous in churches in Addis, and perhaps elsewhere, too. The *senbete* feast always reminds me of the legendary biblical last supper setting we see so often in pictures/drawings. The difference would be that in the *senbete* case, members of the clergy, larger in number than the biblical disciples, would instead occupy the benches for the meal. The long table (imagine a dozen picnic tables joined together) along a same-sized long bench would form parallel columns in the *senbete* hall. What used to amaze me then was that the priests, deacons and other members of the clergy would be seated first and served food and local beer (*tella*). As a side bar, it was a funny spectacle to watch some priests getting slowly transformed from an absolute calm into a tipsy and talkative mood as the benign and but mildly alcoholic *tella* works its way through their system. Be that as it may, it was only after everybody else was served and contented that the "*famished*" members of the *senbete mahiber* would get to sit and eat. I think that was the whole idea, in hindsight. The perk (if I may use the word) that members would extract from this, was a guarantee that they would be given a burial spot in the *senbete* compound, in addition to, of course, fulfilling their Christian*ly* duties. My late father used to belong to such a *senbete mahiber*. The members would prepare meals aplenty and take them to the *senbete* hall, housed in the church compound of St. Emanuel's Church, which was only a stone-throw distance from our house in *Addis Ketema,* AA. My task (along with my late brother and others) was to carry the food, bread and *tella* to the *senbete* premise. One would also have to prepare a special basket of bread (*mesob*) and a pot-ful (*genbo*) of *tella* (the "scared" *Tswa* duo) covered with bright and multi-colored cloth, which would then be handed over to the next household scheduled to prepare the next feast the following agreed-upon *St's* day. The designated household would receive the sacred *Tswa* with an *il'lta* jubilation. The cycle would continue.

I used to enjoy every bit of the ceremony. Many, many years later (1970's), St. Emanuel's Church was renovated to a magnificent structure, thanks to generous monetary donations from its devoted and kind congregation. May I dare say that those were "innocent" communal days!

ግጥሞቼና ትዝታዎቼ   ፈቃዱ ፉላስ

The Abortive *Coup d'état* of B/General Mengistu Neway

We used to call him just "*shambel*." He was an officer in the Imperial Body Guard prior to, and during B/Gen. Mengistu's abortive *coup d'etat* of 1960. I will return to my recollection of him in a second.

I'm sure other folks have a clearer and more informed memory of the events of that momentous time than a 7- or 8-year old at the time has. All this infantile and fallible child of the time remembers of that ill-fated Thursday is his sprinting home from the then-newly built *Leul* Mekonnen School, whose gates were flung wide-open in a confused hurry to let pupils out. Horse-drawn carts (*garis*) were almost airborne flying at a dazzling speed in the direction of *Kolfe*. *Kolfe* was a *gari* station, where the riders used to water, clean up their horses, readjust and reinforce their cart accessories. I remember the deafening sound of bullets in the air. It was the opening salvo of the coup. A short distance, I and my late brother sprinted home safe and sound. Of course, author Greenfield in his voluminous book has captured all the minute and intimate details of the background, the course and the aftermath of the *coup de'tat*. I happened to revisit his book recently; it transported me back to that time. Well, my purpose in this email is not to dissect the movement; but rather, to call up my memory of the time as I exactly remember it from the tiny *sefer*'s vantage point.

In our neighborhood (*sefer*) in *Addis Ketema*, there were two soldiers widely known to the *sefer*---a private in the Army (in the transport unit) [*Mersha*] and a captain in the Imperial Body Guard (*Tadesse*). It is to be recalled that the Army and the Guard stood opposing each other at the later stage of the coup. I recall the army person (*torse*) was a relative of ours, while *shambel* was adored and loved by the *sefer* community. In fact, his wife (dripping in jewelry from ears to toes---stands out in my memory) partook in the same monthly St. Mary's day feast (*mahber*) with my late mother. Each *mahiber* member household would prepare nice meals (traditional style, of course) on a rotation basis every St Mary's day. Used to escort my mother every month to these household feasts to enjoy the delicious food. No chairs and tables in those days; seating for the feast was on a mat on the floor. Looking back, the simplicity was indeed amazing and earthly. On the specific occasion of the *shambel's* household turn, *shambel* would go around pouring *tella* and *araqe* in the glasses of the floor-seated lady *mahberetgnas*--- unheard of in those days, for a guy of his status at the time. That was, thinking back, what made him adorable.

The coup changed the neighborhood (*sefer*) dynamics, especially as it related to the families of *Mersha* and *Taddese*. The *mahiber* was also suspended indefinitely. Toward the conclusion of the coup, *shambel* was rounded up at his house and imprisoned--later on pardoned. *Mersha* quit the Army eventually. Both had passed away since and faded away in time except in my memory. The *sefer* was robbed off its innocence--positive or negative, I don't know even to this day.

Studying in Churches and at Cemeteries

Who amongst that generation in the good old days had not grabbed a handful of class notebooks and textbooks to "study" in what I call *Nature's Library*—church premises, the woods and cemeteries? I had on my part, in my ever-unquenchable thirst to soak up knowledge and score decent *"marks"* in the nerve-twisting and yet enjoyable tests and finals. This happened more frequently in my elementary school days. Two churches stand out---St. *Raguel* Church in the womb of *Merkato* and St. Emanuel Church at the western flanks of *Addis Ketema,* Addis Ababa. The idea behind choosing *Nature's Library* was to immerse oneself, without distraction, in the tranquil and soothing environment that those reclusions provided. The irony of it was that, *Raguel* Church, nestled in the hustle and bustle of *Merkato*, still provided a sanctuary for worshippers, and a secluded haven for us then-kids to hit the books under the shade of magnificent and giant sycamore trees of the church compound.

The woods (*chak'a*)-library was a different matter, though. You would first find a spot and then clear up the ground-hugging shrubbery and linas, lest you lied down on you know what! If you are lucky enough, you would also be in the vicinity of *Nature's Food Store* (*agam* and *qega* plants), and you'd all be set for a delicious snack right there from *Nature's* gracious shelf. All you got to do was just pick them up and eat up to your "seedy" delight. As a side note to the botany-minded, let me point out that the Latin binomial for *agam* is *Carissa edulis*, and that for *qega* is *Rosa abyssinica*. Oh *Father Nature*, how nice and kind of *thou* to leave *thine* hidden, serene and aromatic kitchen wide-open to those knowledge-thirsty lads, so that they would not suffer from the gripping fangs and pangs of hunger, while studying hard and furious! Who ever knew the destiny of those little kids? Let it be told that I didn't know mine. My journey, not unique at all, has been replete with peaks of ecstasy and valleys of despair, not necessarily in that order. I digressed; apologies requested.

I confess that cemeteries were never my favorite "*library*," although some childhood classmates preferred them. Cemeteries literally petrified me. I thought the dead would rise and torment me for encroaching upon their forbidden abode! Their abode was not supposed to be tampered with by the "wicked" living, especially by us knowledge-seeking *munchkins*. By the way, bless all souls of the dead! No pun intended here.

"Studying" was accomplished in groups—usually you would pair up with a similar-minded close friend and hit *Nature's Library*. The exercise would involve first "cramming" in solitude, and then joining up for the "*Great Inquisition*," whereby each partner would ask of the other questions from notes. The sequence would continue for a good 2 to 4 hours, by which time the pupils would be satisfied. In between, of course, ribald jokes would be shared as a recess entertainment. Whether this type of learning (I mean, rote memory) was correct or not is a different topic. However, at least it tested how fast and how long one would store and retain information, respectively, in the folders of her/his mental software.

Gizaw the Robin-hood

I'm not sure how the psychology works, but I hope I don't get in trouble if I say that Ethiopians have a proclivity to worshiping "folk" heroes both of the criminal and political types. Of course, a hero to one is a villain to the other, depending on where one stands. Legends are built around such personalities, so much so that they are elevated to a saintly/phantom, *nay* Herculean status. They are credited with achieving big feats, even when they are only remotely linked to events. Have seen many of them in our lifetime, haven't we?

I remember as recent as the *Derg* years, a one-eyed dissident in *Gojam* by the name Ba'mlaku used to invoke terror among the local populace at the very mention of his name. To the *Derg*, he was a villain; to locals he was a hero; in fact, he had had prior fame for courage. Every "feat" used to be attributed to him even when he was far away from the place. That was during the "*Idget Behibret Zemacha*" days. Which brings me to the topic of this series in a much earlier time-frame.

Gizaw Tsegaye was much older than the rest of us kids---say he was about 17 and we were 9 or 10. He was also one "*sefer*" away; nevertheless, contiguous *sefers*. Gizaw's reach was across "*sefers,*" though. I'm talking about residential areas in the *Mercato* quarters of Addis. He never went or rarely went to school. He spent his days planning and executing mischief's. Every kid used to have a little bit of mischief in them. However, the "inconsequential" small mischief's paled when compared to Gizaw's. He considered himself a Robinhood-type hero.

In those days, horse-mounted policemen used to roam around wooded (*Chaka*) areas in *Addis Ketema* to hunt down gambling (*qumartegna*) kids who played games for money---*arbesht, tif tif (zewd/gofer)*, etc. One time, Gizaw was in such an adventure when he was spotted with other kids. All scattered, except Gizaw who managed to knock down the policeman from his horse and rode off on the horse *a la* Robinhood. Eventually, he abandoned the horse and he was never apprehended. On another occasion, he burnt down a make-shift shelter. Some workers were clearing an area of *Eucalyptus* trees. They were clearing the trees to make room for house-building, and in the process sell the dried trees as fuel. Gizaw gathered up his buddies and constructed a bow and an arrow from sturdy sticks and string. He bought some kerosene and lit up the tip of cloth-tipped arrow and shot a couple of them to a distant hut-like temp shelter. Everything caught fire and was bunt to ashes. Gizaw fled the scene and was never apprehended. Thus, the legend continued----when we used to play "marbles = *biy*" Gizaw would suddenly show up to scatter us around like chicken and appropriate our "marble balls." Ladies and gents, my foot!---that was not a character of Robin-hood :)-.

Was the above story pervasive in our political culture, too? I will leave the judgement to readers of "Gizaw the Robinhood" from my memory lane.

Mud-slinging (*Chiqa Wurwera*)

Whenever I hear of the phrase "mud-slinging," it reminds me of my childhood days. It used to happen during my pre-teen years or just about that time. There were a bunch of kids where I grew up, kids stratified into groups by age. The little ones (maybe 6-10 YOA group), the middle (11-13 YOA) and the grown-ups (over 13; so-called teenagers)---that was approximately the age classification we applied without actually knowing it. So, each age group used to band together while playing games (*birr, biy, qorki, shertete, rucha,* and so on), or cooking up (kneading) some noxious childhood mischief.

During the monsoon rainy season (*kiremt*), we used to have "mud fights" against kids of the same age group in the adjacent neighborhood (*sefer*). *Addis Ketema* (in Addis Ababa) was not as populated then as it is now---was plenty of open space (ground) to run around playing soccer or what have you. So, the mud-fight would start between the "warring" camps, each comprising about 20-25 kids. What you would do is roll up wet mud (semi-solid) and fire it with bare hands against "troops" on the other side. A small group in the rear would be suppliers of mud to the "fine" throwers at the front-line. No one was supposed to embed stone or hard stuff within the mud-ball, lest anybody was hurt. The penalty for such foul action was the halt of the fight, which none of the warring groups would want---

after all, it was supposed to be fun. The declared winner would be the one who advanced forward with a barrage of mud balls against a retreating (flying) group. Well, the aftermath of the battle would be residual mud splashes all over corrugated iron fences and outside walls of houses in the neighborhood, which would drive parents up the wall---giving their children a heavy dose of scolding and rebuke. For the kids, after all, it was all fun, fun, fun!!! Not anymore, at least for me---that "mudslinging" business in the metaphoric sense.

Of *Wolde Pastae Bet*

I don't speak Italian nor write it; so, I don't know where the *Amarigna*-adopted word "*pastae*" came from. I assume it was of Italian origin. In any event, it was a childhood delicacy, if you will. Mind you, ladies and gents, I'm reminiscing about the late 1950's and early 1960's. The road to "*duriyenet,*" it was believed by parents then, was through eating *pastae*. Nevertheless, I didn't end up that way, nor did my arteries break wide open due to plaque deposition. The reasoning (for *duryenet*) eludes me to this day, though. It may be that if you couldn't afford it, you would steal money to get it, and then progress through the glorious path of *duryenet* ! Still a mystery.

In any event, there was this popular "*pastae bet*" in *Merkato* ---called *Wolde pastae bet*, named after its owner. A single *pastae* would cost you a hand and a limb, a staggering "*amist santim*!" The size was humongous, dubbed *sefaed ye'miahil*. There would be a furious rush (like the famous American gold rush, I guess!) in the early morning to get it, just as it came out of the deep-frying pan. Maybe, cooking oil was abundant and cheap then. You indulge in one hot piece, washing it down with a glass of hot tea; you were done for the day. Was so filling, tell you! Of course, there were *pastae bets* all over town, some more popular than others. *Wolde's*, however, was peerless--shall I dare say!

The day I lost the Coffee Beans

I was 9 or 10 years old. My routine, along with my late brother, was to escort our mother on her end-of-the-day open-market shopping to fix dinner for the family and brew some coffee. Along the way, as a reward we would get treated to crunchy bread sticks at a bakery stop on our way home. Our task was to carry the hand-woven basket (*zenbil*) into which our mother would place her groceries. The daily grocery list wouldn't run that long---usually would comprise some onions, spices, cooking oil, salt and coffee beans.

The coffee beans, she would place in a handkerchief, securely tie it, and carefully put it in the basket. Well, it turned out that day I was the one to carry the basket with a stern warning from mother to hold on to it tight, lest some thief snatch it out of my hands. Well, we elbowed our way out of the busy open market of *Merkato* behind the current Commercial Bank (the bank didn't exist then). There was a notorious urchin by the name Mulatu (dark and bubbly kid), whose face I remember even today. Almost everybody in *Mercato* knew him. He was a creative and elusive pick-pocket---so young at that time (maybe, he was 13 or 14). All of a sudden it rained, and we (I, my late brother and mom) took shelter under a canopy of a shop to avoid the rain. I remember seeing Mulatu around the corner of my eyes---never occurred to me what he was up to, despite his notoriety. The rain stopped, and headed we were to home. Once at home, it was time to unload the groceries out of the basket---well, every item was accounted for, except one--*lo and behold*, the coffee beans were gone. I replayed what could have happened in my mind, and then knew exactly what took place---it was Mulatu in his usual daily action. I was so embarrassed and angry at myself that it happened to me. I cursed the little devil profusely! Fortunately, there was still some coffee left at home for that night. That was the day I lost the coffee beans.

Reminds me of the penetrating poem "*Ay Merkato*," by the late great Poet Laureate Tsegaye G/Medhin in his compilation"*Isat woi Abeba*." How true!

The Primers and March of Time

Who, amongst that generation, doesn't remember the soft-covered Primers, so-called Green Primer, Red Primer, and so forth? If memory doesn't fail me, I believe it started with the Green Primer, which had the Aladdin story---who went to China to bring a Lamp------and so forth. The Primers were in the English learning series. We used to memorize the lines. A lot of captivating short stories in the series, at least to our "green" mind then!

Then in the Social Studies, there was this famous "March of Time" book, which was a hard-cover and half-pictorial. The cover was orange-red---I can still picture it in my rear-view mental binoculars. It had stories about Hannibal, Alexander the Great and the Roman Empire. As kids we used to be mesmerized by the stories of the warriors and empire builders. To our mind then, they appeared to be invincible. Looking back, one is left wondering how little, if at all, we were taught about our own colorful history. Maybe, we were entering the Era of Enlightenment *via* European history. Well, one can dissect the reasons, and if that was indeed true---that is a different story. What is the point in all this, you may ask? Not really much; one just calls it "reminiscing" for whatever it is worth.

The Mill House (*Wefcho Bet*)

They called it "*weftcho bet.*" Nobody knows who first christened it with that name. But definitely it was students! Theories abound why it was so named. One is that the hallway used to collect a lot of dust blown in from outside; the second theory was that it was shaped like "*weftcho bet.*" Be that as it may, it was a free-standing one-floor building reserved for matriculating students at Prince Mekonnen High School in *Addis Ketema* (Addis Ababa). I had the "unique" and "historic" opportunity along with my classmates to be one of the earliest inhabitants of that structure in the late 1960's. I remember we felt special and privileged to be secluded from the rest of the buildings. Looking back, not really a privilege to speak of. Around the corner of this structure, students meandered to share cigarettes and morning gossips before the class of the day started. The irony of it all was that when you sat in the class, you could hear students talking loud outside in the alley. Some teachers used to be bothered by it, others not so much.

    As a side bar, we had one funny teacher for whom politicking meant everything. He overused the name "*joro tebi.*" Students used to be amused by his sense of politics. On one occasion, he really wrestled to get across to the class what he deemed was a big "political dynamite." He made the whole class anxious and restless to hear what he had up his sleeves---that *tsunami*-like shocker which would rattle (agitate) all of us. Alas, he told us what it was in a rhetorical way! "Why are you students required to pay fees for text-books?" he asked. That was it; no more. The class was waiting for the big jolt---nothing came. I remember students chuckling and laughing over the huge revelation! By the way, students had known about the case, prior to the "revelation." It was nothing close to a "shocker."

Of Parties

He was a party guy, not the political kind of party. I mean like the merry dance-the-day (or -night)-away sort of party. His name was Tesfaye Yeaine Abeba. The years were in the 1960's--organizing dance parties were turning vogue both for the mere earthly pleasure of it, and later even as a money-making venture. Tesfaye was one of a kind in that department. He was a so-so student, but when it came to organizing dance parties, he was at the pinnacle of it. The dance parties would be organized in private houses, and for "smart" people like Tesfaye at hot spots like *La Mascotte*---which was down by the street leading to Addis Ababa (then HSI) Football Stadium. Tesfaye almost made it like a business. He would collect money from party-goers to rent a place, and eventually would make money after paying out all his expenses. Of course, there were always the usual skirmishes between groups who would "invade" these parties to seek out gang rivals to avenge a past adverse encounter. In a way, the parties were not always a joyful experience---at times they were dreaded because of knifings that resulted in casualties---sustaining knife wounds was not uncommon. The so-called "*China Group*" headquartered in *Merkato* was the most ferocious of them all. Their membership was big---hence the name. The 1974 political tsunami effectively ended this decadent youth culture, maybe in a positive way, sort of. Tesfaye exited the "party organizing business" long before things trended the ugly way.

Sugar (*Wonji Sikuar*)

Remember "*Wonji s'ikuar*?" It used to be packed in small plastic sacs, bearing an elephant emblem. As a kid, I remember those VW vans ("*kumbi*" Volkswagens) cruising the streets of Addis Ababa with a blaring loudspeaker mounted on them. A huge elephant sign would be painted on the van, just like the one on the tiny packet to signify that *Wonji* sugar would make you as strong as an elephant. The announcement from the loudspeaker would run to the effect---drink *Wonji* sugar, it would make you as strong as an elephant. I had had a friend who would run to a tiny kiosk (*su'q*), buy a packet, and gulp down the contents in one serving, as a loyal reaction to the advert. Cavities, dental caries, obesity, precipitating hyperglycemic episodes were not at all a concern in those days. We all had the sweetest of teeth, didn't we? Who would care about medical issues, anyways! They were unheard of, or if heard of, they were just lunatic ideas.

Kur Kur

I am not sure how many remember "*Kurkur*" on the streets of Addis. At any given time, it would seat about three people, excluding the driver, if memory has not failed me. I think the name was given to it because of the typical noise it made, while cruising the thoroughfares of Addis Ababa. It was rather a three-wheeled motor-bike variant, but fully covered with canvas-like material. It was cheaper to ride a *kurkur* than a taxi-cab. It used to be a special treat when my late father would take us his small children to "*Filwuha*" (to bathe) in a *kurkur*. Over the years, it became extinct---don't know how and why. I hear that it has already made a big comeback under a new name, *Bajaj*.

Speaking of Siberia

It was the coldest spot on the whole Haile Selassie I University (HSIU) campus planet. I'm writing about the prefab (short for prefabricated) dorm at *Sidst Kilo*. The structure was made from steel. Actually, it can be likened to a cooler. This "toddler" soul was a freshman in 1970, and he had the "unique and distinctive privilege" of being an Eskimo in an otherwise tropical climatic belt, if you will. He was a Life Science student at *Arat kilo*, but as luck would have it, he was assigned to "Siberia" for dormitory.

By comparison, I repeat by comparison, *Menelik*, *Asfawossen* and *Mekonnen* Residence Halls at *Arat Kilo* were exquisite, or shall I say palatial? Then, there was *Itege wot bet* (not unimpressive by prefab standards) on the shoulder of *Sidst Kilo* campus, across a street, where his high school buddies from Prince Mekonnen High School (PMHS) were assigned---he used to envy them. Good grief, do not let your bare body touch the steel railing of the double-decker in the morning hours! You would otherwise recoil from the stinging sensation---it would be, so to speak, your alarm clock; yes, your alarm clock!

Tearooms

When I was growing up in Addis Ababa, tearooms were our best past-time spots. They were aplenty around town; they were a notch higher than "ፓስቴ" and "ሳምቡሳ" houses. In *Merkato*, Mohammed Salah and *Africawuyan* tea rooms stood out in the mid-1960's. California tearoom was right under our nose, a few blocks away from our school (PMS). It predated others a little bit and was relatively small. Forget about sugar-laden pastries (cakes) in shops; were either scanty or a bit pricey. Tea would be served in a tiny dark blue kettle on a tray, surrounded by a bunch of what looked like shot glasses, but less sturdy. It used to be called "በራድ ሻይ", but considering the fact that it was hot tea, I don't know how "በራድ" was derived. It may have other etymological roots. In any event, the tea would be shared by a bunch of us kids. What stands out in my memory was that there was no subject considered a taboo to be talked about; ranged from juvenile politics, economics, sports, adventures, great escapades to ribald jokes and what not. If you had extra money you would also order ፉል (cooked and buttered kneaded beans), ፈታ (bread crumbs with milk curdle and butter), or ናሼፍ (again spiced and butted bread crumbs). To our olfactory/organoleptic senses then, they were all delicious and to "die for." Ladies and gents, the chariot of time had wheeled off, out of town long time ago; yet the memory lives on with this chap.

Amin Hanna

Venting nostalgia of "olden" days once in a while is therapeutic of sorts, they say. So, here I go. His name was Amin Hana. Rumor had it then that he was an army general in Egypt in the wake of the meteoric rise to power of Gamal Abdel Nasser. He fled Egypt and took refuge in Ethiopia, where he ended up being a Unit Leader (today's equivalent of Assistant Director) at the former Prince Mekonnen School (PMS) in the lovely city of Addis. He was known, nay feared, as a strict disciplinarian, maybe a carryover trait from his military days. It took a huge intestinal fortitude to discipline kids at PMS, especially when not executed well. His wholesale misconception sometimes landed him at loggerheads with many a student. That may be a story unto itself for another time. For now, I recount about my own experience.

    I had an unpleasant encounter with him, which exposed his misguided rage. I was a fully grown-up kid in Grade 10 as can be imagined. It was customary in those days to get a permission slip from a teacher and take a visit to an on-campus clinic. Granted, some of course abused the privilege and instead went to the soccer field to relax or for simple meandering. On that particular day, I was not feeling well in my stomach and had to seek permission from none other than my favorite English teacher Mr. Malik, whose class I would never miss for the world. However, I was so sick that morning that I had to get his permission to go to the clinic. I stepped out of the classroom and was in the hallway heading to the clinic two floors down. Mr. Hanna sneaked behind me and without asking a single question of me just slapped me in the face. Confused and angry, I wanted to return the favor in kind, but some-how I held myself in check. I was not prepared for it and just froze. I headed back to the classroom with him, where he had the confirmation from Mr. Malik that I had indeed secured his permission. I didn't want to go to the clinic again that morning and decided to tough it out—did suck it up big time until the end of the school day. Two years later, when I matriculated, I had to go to his office to get my ESLCE results, which were not shabby by any measure. While he was looking at the certificate and then my face (back and forth), I saw in his eyes a sense of guilt about what had happened two years earlier. I didn't utter a word, yet from the bottom of my heart and the deep recess of my soul, I forgave him, although I never forgot the incident. Ladies and gents, that was some 49 years ago. Looking back now, I understand and can somewhat rationalize the standards of the time, right or wrong-----the incident might not have been typical. If I met him today, I would probably hug him and feel sorry for him. He is no more, I presume! The memory, though, lives on until the proverbial curtain of "time" falls down before my eyes on the precarious "stage" of drama-like poetic life—once and for all, that is!

Camping Tent

A memory that stands out in my mind was the experience I had as a Boy Scout in my elementary school days at *Wossen Seged* School in Addis. As a Boy Scout, I used to enjoy being decked out in khaki clothes adorned with a green scarf, a hat and a utility knife for emergent purposes. One time, a bunch of us (15 or so Boy Scouts) went on a camping trip to a wooded area at the outskirts of Addis near *Aqaqi*. We were supposed to have some fun and partake in some activities. One such activity would be how to leave track of yourself with sticks from the woods, so that somebody could find you easily, in case you are lost, etc., etc. Our camping tent was small, worn out and nearing its life-time. All of a sudden, our patrol leaders came up with a surprise plan--to request the King to grant us a bigger and more spacious tent. The going rationale which would play in our favor was that we were from a school named after his grandson, the son of his favorite son, Prince Mekonnen. The plan for the following day (Saturday) was to be by the road-side on the road to Debre Zeit (DZ), which was the route the Emperor would take for his weekly resting trip to Fairfield Palace in DZ. We were instructed by our leaders to prostrate ourselves in the middle of the road when the motorcade came thru'. Lo and behold, around noonish the lead motorbike-mounted police officer (Bekele Timo) rode ahead of the motorcade to clear the road as it was customary in those days. Soon after, the motorcade came thru'--we did prostrate ourselves big time. I think judging from the fact that we were kids and in uniform, they knew we were harmless. The way the body guards jumped out of the escort cars with their guns drawn was scary, to say the least. In any case, the selected Boy Scout leader read a brief note why we were on the roadside and what we wanted. The side-window of the Emperor's Cadillac was pulled down, and he listened to our request. We were offered a bunch of *Cherealia* biscuits in colorful plastic wrappers. We were told to send a representative to *Gibi* (Palace) to collect the tent at a later date. However, despite repeated trips to the palace by our leaders, nobody would listen to them past the gate. Because of the intervening bureaucracy, I don't think we received the promised tent any time soon. Maybe, a year or so later. Thusly, the story ended--only the distant memory still lurks in my mind.

Honey-wine Houses (*Wusha Geday Tej Bet*)

While growing up in *Merkato*, I used to hear many weird names of *tej bets* ("honey-wine houses"). One such catchy name was "*Wusha geday tej bet*" [dog killer honey-wine house] in the vicinity of Raguel Church. In fact, the story was also once told in a *Merkato* Magazine. Customers of the *tej bet* used to be served lard-laden boiled beef soup (*mereq*). People would have to go in with their own improvised toothpicks to scoop out the lard which would stick to the roof of their mouth after they indulge in it. The purpose of the "*mereq*" was to serve as a cushion to slow down the absorption of the nefarious *tej* from their guts into their system. The downside to it was that it was a source of a heavy dose of cholesterol and nasty fatty acids. One devoted customer, as a result, got very heavy. In one of his stay-ins, he had too much "*tej*", got intoxicated and dared step out of the *tej bet*. There used to be a timid semi-stray, nay homeless, dog at the entrance of the *tej bet*--he used to be treated with left-overs. The drunk chap staggered out and couldn't proceed any further; needed a pause. The dog was lying on a bench at the door. Unbeknownst to him (as a drunk person), and in order to collect himself he sat his heavy body on the poor dog to asphyxiate the latter to death--hence the *tej bet* was christened from "*Emahoy Tej Bet*" to "*Wusha Geday Tej Bet*"--well, at least by its devoted customers. Let it be known to this sober Cosmos that I was not a customer of it; otherwise, I wouldn't have survived to this sunny day!

"*Ay Merkato!*" ---as exclaimed by the late Poet Laureate TGM !!!